Wicked Springfield

Wicked SPRINGFIELD

CRIME, CORRUPTION & SCANDAL DURING THE LINCOLN ERA

Erika Holst

THE History PRESS

Published by The History Press
Charleston, SC 29403
www.historypress.net

First published 2010

Manufactured in the United States

ISBN 978.1.59629.901.6

Holst, Erika.
Wicked Springfield : crime, corruption, and scandal during the Lincoln era / Erika Holst.
p. cm.
Includes bibliographical references.
ISBN 978-1-59629-901-6
1. Crime--Illinois--Springfield--History--19th century--Anecdotes. 2. Corruption--Illinois--Springfield--History--19th century--Anecdotes. 3. Scandals--Illinois--Springfield--History--19th century--Anecdotes. 4. Criminals--Illinois--Springfield--History--19th century--Anecdotes. 5. Lincoln, Abraham, 1809-1865--Anecdotes. 6. Springfield (Ill.)--History--19th century--Anecdotes. 7. Springfield (Ill.)--Biography--Anecdotes. 8. Springfield (Ill.)--Social conditions--19th century--Anecdotes. I. Title.
HV6795.S67H65 2010
364.109773'56--dc22
2009050778

CONTENTS

Contents

INTRODUCTION

This book is not about Abraham Lincoln and his virtues. It is about Lincoln's hometown and its vices. Lincoln arrived in Springfield, Illinois, in the spring of 1837 as an up-and-coming young lawyer with all his worldly possessions tucked into two saddlebags. Springfield was up-and-coming, too: it had just been selected the permanent capital of Illinois by the state legislature. The town, like the entire West (and Illinois was considered the West in Lincoln's time), hummed with promise, attracting politicians, lawyers, merchants, farmers, ladies, craftsmen and innumerable others in search of possibility and prosperity. It also attracted drifters, con artists, roustabouts and criminals in search of mischief or an easy mark; the editor of the Springfield *Illinois Republican* worried that the new state capital would bring rowdyism and brawling to the streets. By the time Lincoln departed in February 1861 as the newly elected president of the United States, Springfield had had its share of scandals, crimes, brawls and intrigues.

Wickedness came in all forms in Lincoln's Springfield. As capital, it was always a hotbed of politics, and sometimes that bed got too hot for comfort. Candidates often hurled insults and accusations at one another. Occasionally they hurled fists. And every so often, they hurled something deadlier. Being elected to office was no cure for wrongdoing, either. Illinois' long tradition of crooked governors goes all the way back to Lincoln's day.

This is not to say that politicians cornered the market on scandal. There were plenty of everyday citizens who ran afoul of the law and committed crimes that ran the gamut from murder to sexual deviancy, not to mention the

Abraham Lincoln's Springfield, Illinois. *Courtesy of the Sangamon Valley Collection, Lincoln Library, Springfield, Illinois.*

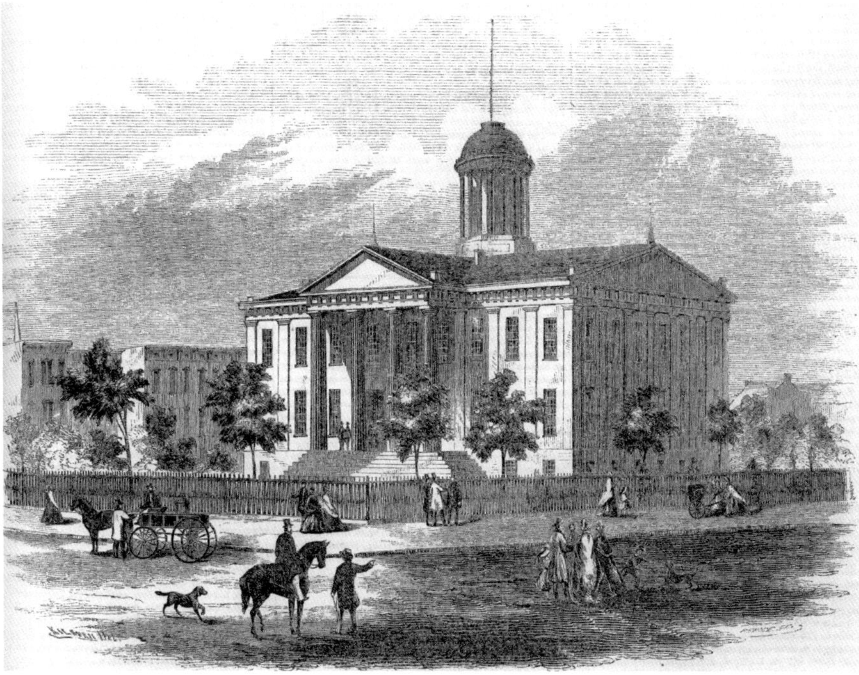

Abraham Lincoln arrived in Springfield the same year it was named Illinois' new state capital. *Courtesy of* Ballou's Pictorial Drawing-Room Companion, *November 15, 1856.*

handful of citizens who stayed on the right side of the law but nevertheless kept African Americans in slavery or near slavery. Right there in the Great Emancipator's hometown.

Lincoln even had a scandal of his own, back in his early days before time and experience smoothed away some of his rough edges. He had the bad habit of making personal attacks on his political rivals, using humor and mockery to "skin" people who often had no sense of humor when it came to their own shortcomings. That is, until one of his humorless victims had enough and challenged him to a duel.

Although Lincoln was by and large innocent of any wicked or salacious acts, he was surely aware when they were committed in his town. The stories in this book filled the newspapers that he read and the court docket in which he practiced law. Oftentimes the people involved were his legal clients. Sometimes they were his friends or political allies. All of it was part of the fabric of the community in which Lincoln lived. Welcome to Abraham Lincoln's wicked Springfield.

Chapter 1

POLITICAL BRAWLS

Politics dominated the cultural landscape of Lincoln's Springfield in a way that can scarcely be imagined today. Andrew Jackson's brand of democratic politics had opened the door wide to popular participation. No longer were candidates nominated by cabals of political elites and quietly elected by propertied men. In the new era of the common man, politics became a rollicking, contentious, boisterous affair.

Lincoln arrived in Sangamon County at the dawn of this new political era. By the late 1830s, the citizens of Springfield and the surrounding countryside were fiercely divided into two political parties, the Whigs and the Democrats. Whigs believed in an economic policy built around "internal improvements" such as roads, canals and railroads. They favored a protective tariff on American goods and a strong national bank. They idealized their leader, Henry Clay, and loathed their chief opponent, Andrew Jackson. Lincoln was a Whig. Democrats, by contrast, were less interested in modernizing the country's interior than they were in expanding its borders westward. They were opposed to the national bank and to anything smacking of elitism and favored of the "common man."

Political meetings of this time had something of a holiday feel. A typical rally would draw hundreds or thousands of citizens from the surrounding area to wave banners and listen to speeches and debates, eat barbecue, visit with neighbors and heckle opponents.

Newspapers were also cornerstones of the political culture. The concept of objectivity in reporting was unheard of. Rather, most towns had at least two

Politics in Lincoln's time stirred up strong—occasionally violent—feelings. *Courtesy of* Harper's Monthly, *November 7, 1857.*

newspapers, Democrat and Whig, each fiercely loyal to its party and utterly scornful of its rival. A meeting heralded as a great success drawing thousands of spectators by the Whig paper might be dismissed as a fizzle attended by a few dozen morose souls by the Democratic paper. Most politicians were on excellent terms with the editors of their party's paper and often contributed anonymous editorials or pseudonymous letters—a practice Lincoln engaged in frequently and that occasionally landed him in hot water.

Occasionally, political feelings ran too hot and trouble ensued. All too often, a political barb would cross the line into a personal insult, and all too often a violent reaction would result. What follows are three of the most memorable political brawls from Lincoln's Springfield.

FIGHTING WITH WORDS

In 1834, Abraham Lincoln was postmaster at New Salem, Illinois, a little town twenty miles northwest of Springfield. One of the perks of this job was that he could read all the newspapers that came through the office for free before handing them off to their intended recipients. One can picture him in June of that year, feet up on the desk, apple in hand, enjoying the latest copy of someone else's *Sangamo Journal* to pass the time. He'd skim past the advertisements for goods from Philadelphia and a new livery stable on page one, read the news from Congress on page two and sit up and pay particular attention to the letter reprinted on page three—the one that accused the front-runner in the congressional race for his district (and Lincoln's own choice for office) of being a seducer, burglar and general letch.

William L. May and Benjamin Mills were vying to represent the largest congressional district in Illinois, which stretched from Springfield to the Wisconsin border, covering nearly half the state. Both men were Democrats, both were lawyers, both were supporters of Jackson and both had traveled around the district together, campaigning more or less amiably. In fact, by June, Mills and May had mutually agreed that no further campaigning was necessary. "I have entered into an agreement with my opponent that we should each rest our own prospects on the efforts already made," May said. Mills's supporters, however, failed to get the memo that the active campaign was over. In late June, they published a letter in the *Sangamo Journal* raising some unsavory questions about May's past.

The letter's writer, who signed himself only as "Illinois," conscious of the importance of integrity and good character for men serving in high political office, inquired politely if there was any truth to the rumors he had heard: Had May really seduced a young woman by the name of Isabel Rainer in 1825, reneged on his promise to marry her and then tried to buy her off with an old horse and side saddle when she sued him for breach of contract? Had he later gone to a boardinghouse and started courting a young woman, passing himself off as a bachelor when really he had been married for months? And had he really been indicted by a grand jury for burglary when he was living in Edwardsville some years back? Because if he had, perhaps he should step aside and let a more honorable man go to Congress.

May's response was swift and furious. He bought himself three full columns of the *Sangamo Journal* for his reply, paying advertiser's rates, and unleashed a bitter and abusive tirade that, ironically, served only to highlight his lechery rather than quell suspicions about his moral character.

Maybe he had seduced Isabel Rainer, he admitted, not in so many words, but as a youth he had had an "ardent temperament" that led him to many "follies and indiscretions" now thoroughly repented; and anyway, she had "erred" just as much as he had. The bigger crime was on the part of "Illinois," whose "depraved and vitiated appetite for falsehood, detraction, and slander" caused him to go ahead and publish for the entire world to see that Isabel Rainer, now wife, mother and Baptist, had enjoyed naughty carnal pleasures with May outside the bonds of marriage. Why drag her name through the mud; why open old wounds long ago healed?

As to the little matter of being a lodging house lothario, May countered with a statement from the supposed "source" of the rumor. Presumably May would have preferred a slam-dunk refutation, but he had to settle for a tepid letter declaring that the source was "not in possession of any evidence which would in any wise go to substantiate the charge in which I was referred to; and if said charge is substantiated other testimony will have to be procured." Not exactly a ringing rebuttal, but at least the ball was in the accuser's court to produce more evidence.

May reserved most of his wrath for the charge of burglary. A burglar breaks into a house with the intent to *steal*, he thundered. All he had done was sneak into a house in the middle of the night and (inexplicably) put his hand on a man's face, and for that people somehow got the idea that he had broken into the house to commit murder! But that wasn't the case at all—he wasn't a murderer. He wasn't even a burglar. And he could prove it, with a letter from his friend A.W. Cavalry, who loyally testified that, so far as he could tell, "your entry into the dwelling house was not to commit murder, but to have illicit intercourse with a female then residing there." Yes! There you had it. He had only broken into the house to have illicit intercourse with his friend's wife. Not to *murder* anyone, for heaven's sake. How dare they? He finished up his blustering defense by reprinting a letter written on his behalf to Andrew Jackson for a federal appointment, clearly implying that no burglar or suspected murderer could merit such a recommendation.

The opposition, as one might guess, was not about to ignore all of the ammunition May unwittingly handed them. A second letter appeared in the next week's paper, this time signed "Agricola" and dripping with scorn. You protest too loudly, Agricola noted, when you should have "answered coolly, without lashing yourself into a whirlwind of passion, and hurling the epithets and slang about you without aim or direction. What necessity was there, sir, of calling upon the great name of Andrew Jackson to protect you?" Then, with the unerring accuracy of a hawk striking a field mouse, Agricola zeroed in on the massive target May had painted on his own back.

Let me get this straight, Agricola said. You say "I did break into the dwelling house of my friend in the night time, not to commit a felony, to steal 10 pounds of Bacon, or to murder any one, as the young man supposed who awoke and found my fingers to his throat, but only, my dear constituents, *only* to commit adultery with my friend's wife"? And this from a man who had been something of a lowlife in town ("your name became a bye-word, your touch was contamination, your foot-tread was like the mildew"), and the friend whose wife he bedded was one of the few people to take pity on him and let him under his roof. Moreover, he did it at the tender and impressionable young age of…thirty, when he was a widower with two children. "If you, sir, plead at thirty that you have not attained sufficient discretion to be answerable for your acts," Agricola finished up, "you will excuse the voters of the 3d Congressional District, if they should be so perverse as to think that he who is a boy at thirty is not at forty a man."

If shouting is the next best thing to being right, name-calling must be the next best thing to shouting, for it was the defense May then chose to employ. Apparently unable to deny the fact that he did sneak into a house in the middle of the night to sleep with his friend's wife, he went on the offensive. "Who is this 'Agricola?'" he roared in another newspaper response. "Some *puling*, sentimental, *he* old maid! Whose cold liver and pulseless heart, never felt a desire which could be exempted, except for getting money…some spindle-shanked, toad-eating, man-granny, who feeds the depraved appetites of his patrons with gossip and slander…who being deprived of their virility endeavor to compensate themselves by the enjoyments of mischief-making."

Apparently, the one thing Illinois voters liked less than an adulterer was a man-granny. A few weeks later, May was elected to Congress by a comfortable majority. One of his votes came from Abraham Lincoln, who served as a clerk at his election day polling place. May would serve two more successive terms before being ousted from his party's nomination by the political maneuverings of Stephen A. Douglas in 1838. Forced out of national politics, he got himself elected mayor of Springfield and resumed the practice of law, where he would meet eight times in the courtroom the young former postal clerk who once kept tabs on him through the newspaper. One can imagine Lincoln, with his magnanimity and great good nature, was kind enough to overlook the dirty laundry that May blithely hung out to dry that eventful summer of 1834.

FIGHTING WITH FISTS

In the summer of 1838 a clock peddler, making his way through central Illinois, stopped for the night at a hotel in Hancock County with a friend. The innkeeper showed them to a room with two beds, a rare luxury on the frontier where sharing beds with friends—and strangers—was a common occurrence. Their good fortune was not to last, however; in the middle of the night they were roused by the innkeeper, who had two men in tow.

"Sorry to wake you," he apologized, "but these men need a place to sleep. You two either need to sleep together or share your beds with them." The men, he explained, were opposing candidates for Congress. The peddler turned over, rubbed his eyes and beheld a stocky man standing barely more than five feet tall, possessed of a very large head topped with an impressive mane of dark hair. His companion was tall, elegant, with the educated air of a college professor. Both of them waited expectantly for their sleeping arrangements. "Well," said the peddler, "My friend is a Whig, and I am a Democrat." The shorter man considered this information. "You take the Whig, and I'll take the Democrat," he said finally to his companion. With that, they got into bed with their newfound political allies and fell fast asleep. The shorter man was Stephen A. Douglas, current Register of the Land Office in Springfield and future rival of Abraham Lincoln for the hand of Mary Todd, a seat in the Senate and presidency of the United States. The taller man was John T. Stuart, Lincoln's law partner, the man who had fought alongside Lincoln in the Black Hawk War, served with him in the Illinois legislature and first encouraged him to study law.

Both men were running for the same seat in Congress that William L. May had won four years earlier. They had been traveling together across the huge district, which encompassed twenty-two counties from Springfield to Chicago, campaigning and debating, rivals on the stump by day and bedfellows in the rustic country accommodations at night. All told, they spent five months in the saddle, plodding down roads not more than bridle paths, fording streams and rivers in the absence of bridges and sharing lumpy cornhusk mattresses in squalid taverns.

Douglas was twenty-four years old. His extreme youth, already something of a target for ribbing, was not helped by his tiny size. People later recalled that his arms and legs seemed disproportionately short, although his body, one writer later recalled admiringly, was "full and round, as though it never lacked the juices that supply life." Brilliant, ambitious and a terrific public

Lincoln's rival, Stephen A. Douglas, sparred with John T. Stuart on the Market House lawn after a debate. *Courtesy of Library of Congress, Prints and Photographs Division.*

speaker, he was a rising star in the Democratic Party. He had come to Illinois from New England in 1833 and was admitted to the bar the next year. From there, his career skyrocketed: he was named state's attorney in 1835, elected to the state legislature in 1836 and appointed Register of the Land Office in 1837. By 1838, the only person standing between him and the head of the Illinois Democratic Party was Congressman William L. May, the very man who had recommended him for the Land Office. Douglas hated him. Putting his political acumen to work, Douglas organized a Democratic convention in 1838 to have May ousted and himself nominated to run for Congress. He was the Democrats' golden boy, their "high combed cock," their "little giant," and he was ready to go to Congress.

Douglas's opponent, John Todd Stuart, was a long-limbed, well-born Kentucky native, a cousin to the powerful Todd clan of Lexington that included Mary Todd. He had settled in Springfield in 1828 and immediately began a successful law practice. After a brief stint in the Black Hawk War (where he first met the promising young Abraham Lincoln), he was elected to the state legislature in 1832. He was reelected in 1834, this time joined in the General Assembly by his friend Lincoln. In 1837, he took Lincoln on as a junior law partner and found in his new associate an enthusiastic political ally. In 1838, Lincoln singlehandedly managed the law firm in Stuart's absence while providing as much support as he could to the campaign. Lincoln wrote a mutual friend in July, "If we do our duty we shall succeed in the congressional election, but if we relax an iota, we shall be beaten." Lincoln looked up to his aristocratic, well-educated senior partner. By contrast, he tried his best to ignore Douglas, slyly asking, "Is'nt that the best mode of treating so small a matter?"

Lincoln's first law partner, John T. Stuart, tangled with Stephen Douglas during the congressional campaign of 1838. *Courtesy of Frank E. Stevens's* The Black Hawk War, *1903.*

Politically, Stuart and Douglas were fierce rivals. Party politics had divided Springfield squarely into Whig and Democrat camps. The congressional seat up for grabs had most recently been occupied by a Democrat, as had all the state's important political offices for many years past. Douglas was eager to retain this seat for his party and to solidify the hold the Democrats, with their love of the common man and hatred of the national bank, had on the state of Illinois.

But the Whigs, champions of internal improvements and high protective tariffs, felt something stirring on the breeze. The first and second districts were a lost cause, but many Whig settlers were pouring into the third district, placing a congressional seat within reach for the first time in their party's history. Beyond that, hopes were high that a Whig could capture the White House in 1840, and the party faithful were chomping at the bit to begin the political battle. By the time Stuart and Douglas started their race in 1838, Illinois was already in a high state of political excitement—people turned out en masse for meetings, newspapers were started for the sole purpose of trumpeting the party line and politics dominated most every conversation.

Personally, Stuart and Douglas probably got on well enough at the start of things. Springfield was a small place; they knew the same people and moved in the same circles. Both were frequent visitors to the home of Ninian W. Edwards, Stuart's cousin-in-law and the town's social leader. Douglas was jovial and fun-loving; Stuart was intelligent and interesting. But even the most congenial of traveling companions will start to grate on each other's nerves during the long course of a campaign. There is only so much a man can take of being in the exclusive company of his bitterest political rival, only so many greasy meals a man can share at a country inn and only so many corners of bug-ridden mattresses a man can defend against the encroachments of a hairy, snoring bedmate before tempers start to fray. By June, the *Sangamo Journal* was reporting, "It is said that Mr. Douglass' affection for Mr. Stuart is not reciprocated and that Mr. S. has gone south, and will travel no more in his company."

The press did not help matters. The Democratic newspapers chortled that Stuart was too lazy to put his heart into the campaign and that he was a coward who ducked debates rather than embarrass himself against Douglas's superior oratorical talents. The Whig papers fired back that Stuart was perfectly willing to face off with Douglas, only that the "Peoria bantling" (a dig at Douglas's youth and diminutive size) was nowhere to be found. Douglas was sensitive to these cracks about his height. Stuart, in true southern fashion, was fiercely protective of his honor. Each carefully noted the other's vulnerabilities, biding time for the best opportunities to exploit them.

Tensions between the little Democrat and the tall Whig came to a head a few days before the election at a joint debate in front of the old Market House in Springfield. Douglas had the profoundly irritating tendency to accuse his political opponent of things that happened to be unpopular in whichever location they were currently speaking, regardless of whether or not such accusations were true. This he did now, throwing in aspersions against Stuart's character for good measure. Stuart listened, incensed, while Douglas spoke in that intensely aggravating manner of his: haughty, defiant, lip curling with scorn, peppering his speech with offensive language. All of a sudden, something snapped inside Stuart. In an instant he transformed from an elegant, intellectual lawyer to a man hell-bent on kicking Democratic ass…literally.

Jumping up from his seat, he charged forward and seized his opponent around the neck. Douglas was small but scrappy and no doubt put up an admirable fight. Stuart, however, had the advantage of being taller, heavier and severely pissed off. Not content with a mere headlock, Stuart picked Douglas up and carried him about the Market House lawn, while Douglas, sputtering and shouting in protest, flailed desperately in an attempt to free himself. The crowd hooted and hollered to see the little giant carried about like a sack of potatoes, red-faced and shouting, resembling nothing so much as a child in the middle of a tantrum.

Douglas, for his part, did the only reasonable thing a small man in a tough situation could do: he sunk his sharp little Democratic teeth into Stuart's Whiggish thumb as hard as he could. It wasn't a roundhouse punch, but it did the job. With a roar, Stuart dropped Douglas cold and examined his poor,

The Market House, in the center of Springfield, where Douglas and Stuart fought. *Courtesy of the Sangamon Valley Collection, Lincoln Library, Springfield, Illinois.*

bleeding thumb. The flesh was torn like so much raw hamburger. And that was the way that two political giants finished up their campaign for Congress.

Stuart went on to win the election by the very narrowest of margins—after more than thirty-six thousand men had flocked to the polls, Stuart won by a bare seventy-seven votes. When he took his seat in Congress at the next session, his fellow Whigs gave him a standing ovation in salute of his hard-won victory. And a victory it was: for the next decade that seat would remain in Whig hands, including, in 1846, the hands of Abraham Lincoln.

Douglas, for his part, didn't fare too badly. He was eventually elected to Congress in another district and served three terms before being elected to the U.S. Senate.

Stuart carried a scar on his thumb until the day he died as a souvenir of the time he had bested the Little Giant.

FIGHTING (FATALLY) WITH FIREARMS

Campaigns for Congress produced heated tempers and a memorable brawl, but the first office that drove a man to kill in Springfield was something a little less high profile: Register of the Land Office in Galena, Illinois. Well below the national radar, this political plum was nevertheless tantalizing enough to prompt one Democrat to use his pistol on a fellow Democrat (a minister, no less!), giving Abraham Lincoln the chance to cut his teeth as an attorney on the juiciest murder case the town had seen in years.

Henry B. Truett held the coveted office without opposition for a brief, magical time in 1837, during which he enjoyed all of its privileges and perks and all of its land grants to award and land speculation to profit from. He had won the job through the influence of his father-in-law, William L. May, sitting congressman and former enjoyer of illicit intercourse. But May had grown increasingly unpopular with Democrats in Illinois. His opposition to President Van Buren's fiscal policies put him on the wrong side of the party line. Truett, not having much to recommend him other than a well-connected father-in-law, was unpopular, too. At the Democrats' district convention in Peoria, not only was Stephen A. Douglas nominated for the Land Office in question in Truett's place, but the party also added insult to injury by passing a resolution calling for Truett's immediate removal from office. Unfortunately for the author of that resolution, whose liver would bear the full brunt of Truett's rage in the form of a small-caliber bullet fired at close range, Truett was not the kind of man to just bow to the wishes of a convention of his peers.

Professionally, Truett hadn't amounted to much, having tried and failed several occupations before his father-in-law set him up in the Land Office. His lack of actual accomplishment did not stop him from being something of a braggart, however. Lincoln's neighbor, James Gourley, later recalled running a foot race against Truett in 1836 with Lincoln acting as judge.

When Gourley beat Truett, Lincoln was delighted, for "Lincoln loved to see the wind out of the windy fool." Lincoln himself mentioned Truett in unflattering terms in an anonymous January 1838 letter to the *Sangamo Journal*, naming him as the "certain gentleman who resides in Sangamon County, and who has followed a variety of occupations both here and elsewhere, for a living and failed in all," and wondering "when he should be called upon to close up his loafing operations." Finally, like all boastful men with few true talents to boast of, Truett was reputed to be a coward, known to carry pistols around with him wherever he went.

In Truett's defense, a position in the Land Office, unglamorous as it sounds, was very desirable. The Land Office was in charge of the surveying, sale and grants of public lands. It came with a handsome salary and the potential for a shrewd investor to make almost unlimited profits from land speculation. When Douglas served as Register of the Springfield Land Office, a newspaper wryly commented, "We are told the *little man* from Morgan [County], was perfectly astonished, at finding himself making money at the rate of from one to two hundred dollars per day!"

Even more enticing than the office's pecuniary advantages, however, were its political advantages. In a frontier state such as Illinois, with its steady stream of immigrants and skyrocketing land sales, a job in the Land Office brought prestige among local politicians and wide acquaintance with voters. The job was often used as a steppingstone to other, more powerful political positions. Small wonder that Truett was aggrieved at the prospect of losing his coveted job.

The call for his immediate dismissal came in November 1837, eight short months after his appointment. From then until March 1838, though he held on to his office, he also held on to a grudge and quite possibly schemed for revenge. The object of his wrath was Dr. Jacob Early, Methodist minister, railroad contractor and fellow Democrat who, Truett believed, had been responsible for writing the resolution that called for his removal from office.

Their paths crossed on Wednesday, March 7, 1838. Early, who lived four or five miles outside Springfield, had come into town for business and was spending the night at the Spottswood Hotel. (Some years later this same hotel, renamed the Globe, would be home to Abraham and Mary Lincoln during the first year of their marriage.) Unhappily for Early, Truett was in Springfield from Galena on legal business and was also staying at the Spottswood Hotel. Shortly before eight o'clock in the evening, Early settled himself in the hotel's sitting room in front of the fire to read. A number of other gentlemen were in the room, including Truett, who spoke at length

The Spottswood Hotel, later known as the Globe Tavern, where Henry Truett shot and killed Jacob Early. *Courtesy of* Springfield in 1892: Souvenir Supplement, Illinois State Journal, *1892*.

with a business associate. One by one, most of the men drifted out of the room, leaving only Truett, Early and a few onlookers who later recalled Truett staring at his supposed nemesis with an expression disturbing enough to merit notice.

Finished with his book (the last one he would ever read, little did he know), Early moved to a settee and propped up his feet by the fire. Truett, no longer content just to stare, stood, planted himself directly in front of Early and demanded to know whether Early was the author of the hateful resolution that threatened to cost Truett his job. When Early did not answer right away, Truett repeated his question, calling Early a "damned scoundrel" and "damned rascal" for good measure. Early protested against the insults and asked who had told Truett that he was responsible for the resolutions. Truett, getting nowhere with "scoundrel" and "rascal," repeated his question yet again and this time called Early a "damned hypocrite" and "damned coward," presumably hoping this would yield better results. Early, however, was too distracted by the sight of the gun in Truett's coat to make a reply. Instead, he leapt to his feet and took up a chair by the legs, brandishing it out in front of him like a lion tamer. The two circled each other uneasily for a moment, Early trying to keep his assailant at bay, before Truett pulled out his pistol (which witnesses later swore he brought into the room already cocked) and fired. He was standing no more than three feet away from Early, who dropped like a stone, the bullet having pierced his abdomen and torn its way through his liver and lower stomach before exiting though his back.

Early lingered for a few days before dying the following Saturday night. Truett had released the pistol immediately after firing it and fled out the hotel's back door into the night. He didn't get far; within a week he found himself behind bars. It was probably for the best. Early was a popular and beloved citizen, and his murder prompted outrage on the part of Springfield's citizenry, who were clamoring for a hanging. At least in jail Truett was safe from the danger of vigilante justice while he waited for his day in court.

In consideration of the danger of hanging, the case was continued to the fall term of court, and Truett cooled his heels in jail for a full seven months. His trial began on October 8, 1838, in the Sangamon County Circuit Court, which at that time was located in a nondescript office building directly under the law offices of Stuart & Lincoln. The court appointed Stephen A. Douglas as state's attorney *pro tempore* in place of the absent prosecutor. When Daniel Woodson was elected as state's attorney, Douglas turned the case over to him but remained engaged as Woodson's associate. The defense team, assembled by Truett's father-in-law May, consisted of Edward D. Baker, Stephen T. Logan and the partnership of John T. Stuart and Abraham Lincoln. Lincoln at this point had only been practicing law for one year; it was his first murder trial.

It took three full days to select the jury, which was an inordinately long time in that era. By the time the jurors had been settled on, nearly four hundred citizens (one-tenth of the voters in Sangamon County) had been called and rejected. On the fourth day, the proceedings got underway. Truett, pale and twitchy from his lengthy confinement in the county jail, listened as Douglas and Woodson presented the evidence. It seemed like an open-and-shut case: Truett's anger over his removal from office, his coming into the hotel sitting room with a cocked pistol, the creepy way he stared at Early and the way he insulted the much taller and stronger man—all this implied malicious intent to kill.

The defense had a significant mountain of evidence to overcome if they were going to introduce the possibility of reasonable doubt into a case

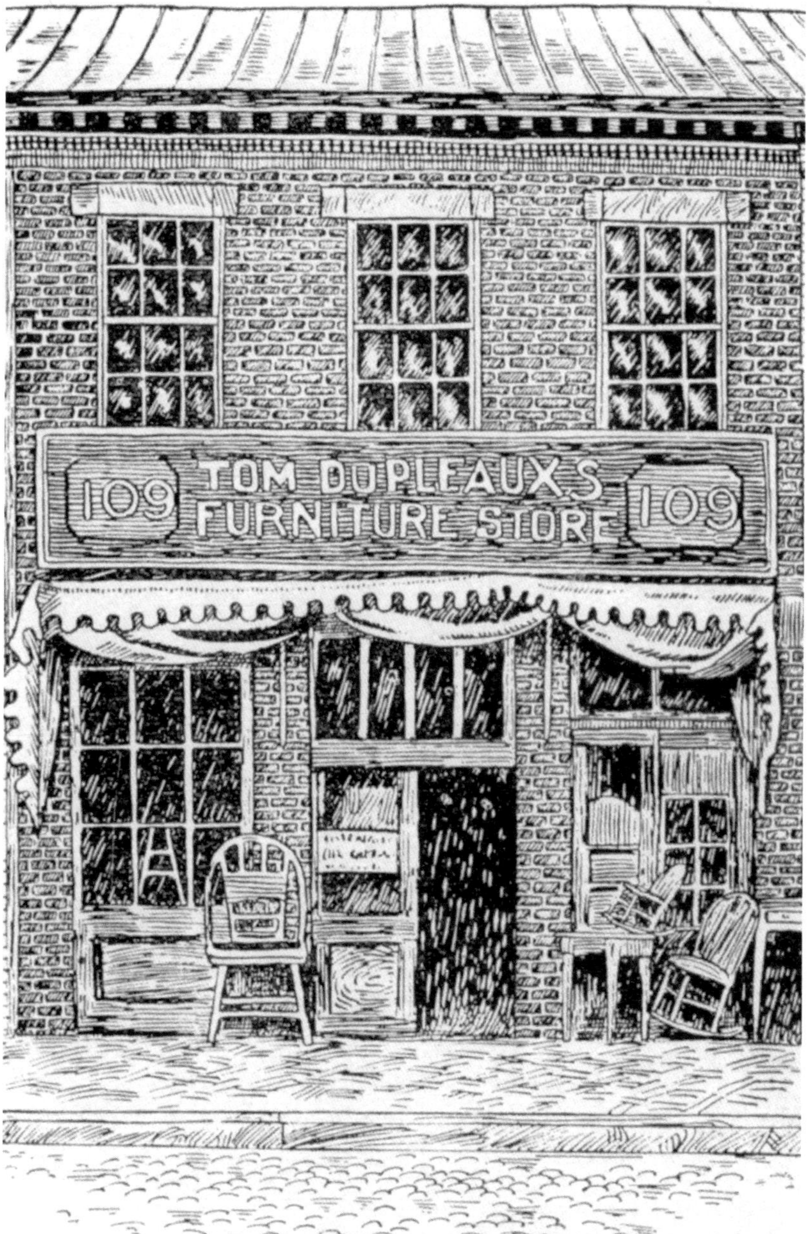

In 1838, this building housed the Sangamon County Circuit Court on the first floor and the law offices of Stuart & Lincoln on the second floor. *Courtesy of Albert Walter Lewis's* Springfield: The Capital of the State of Illinois, *1912.*

where witnesses had observed their client pull the trigger and then run away, literally leaving a smoking gun behind. Fortunately, the late, lamented Dr. Early, by picking up a chair to fend off his assailant, had given them a sliver of opportunity. With nothing to lose, the defense team seized on it. The chair, they contended, was a deadly weapon, and with it in his hands Early, not Truett, was the aggressor. Truett only shot him in self-defense. They wrapped up their argument with a few moving words about the damage done to Truett's honor by being kicked out of office and the discomfort he had suffered by being incarcerated for seven months. Lincoln made the closing argument, delivering what his future law partner Stephen T. Logan called a "short but strong and sensible speech."

The jury retired to Stuart & Lincoln's office to deliberate and, after two hours, came back with their verdict: not guilty. The crowd was stunned and not a little outraged. Truett was overjoyed. Lincoln and his partners were each $250 richer after May paid the legal bill, and Lincoln now had a successful criminal defense under his belt.

After the trial, Truett hightailed it back to Galena and resigned the office that drove him to kill. For a while he worked in a lead mine, and eventually he got himself elected mayor. He may have been acquitted in the eyes of the law, but in the court of public opinion he was guilty as sin, and the newspapers never passed up an opportunity to say so. When he served as delegate to the Democratic Senatorial Convention in 1840, the Whig press called him an "acquitted murderer" and sniffed that "we always knew the mantle of democracy was a broad one, but we cannot yet persuade ourselves that it can cover the heinous sin of murder. For the character of our State, we wish our opponents would pay a little more attention to character." Of course, Truett's continued combativeness made it hard for him to keep a low profile. In 1848, Mayor Truett attacked a man in the street and was "carried off the ground in an insensible state" after being "badly whipped," prompting the *Galena Gazette* to opine, "Mr. T…has not the qualifications essential to the proper discharge of the duties of Mayor, and the feeling is general that he ought to resign."

At some point, having picked all the fights he cared to pick in Illinois, Truett pulled up stakes and headed west to California. The last Springfielders heard of him was a tidbit in the *Illinois State Register* in the fall of 1855: "H.B. Truett, formerly of this state, fought a duel with Ashton E. Smith, at San Francisco, on the 19th ult. Smith was slightly wounded, and Truett's trousers were torn. This is the same Truett who, eighteen years ago, killed Dr. Early, in this city."

Chapter 2

GOVERNORS' (MIS)DEEDS

In Illinois, politics and corruption seem to go hand in hand. Nowhere is this more obviously or embarrassingly apparent than in the governor's office. In the past century, one out of five Illinois governors has been charged with a felony after committing breathtaking examples of malfeasance running the gamut from corruption to fraud, racketeering and embezzlement. As comedian Jon Stewart archly pointed out, one stands a better chance of going to prison by being an Illinois governor than by being a murderer.

Although we sometimes like to think that corruption is a product of modern times and that people in the past had more integrity, Illinois' tradition of political corruption reaches all the way back to Lincoln's Springfield. Law-abiding citizens bemoaned the loss of republican ideals and feared that such corruption would tear the government apart: "When official corruption can go unwhipt of justice, and when it may with impunity stalk forth in open day, with its hideous and monstrous form appearing through its transparent covering, and when courts shall cease to employ every power that the law has conferred upon them, to inflict the severest penalties it has denounced against such crime, then organized society is ready to dissolve, and governments cease to exist," declared one Supreme Court justice in 1860.

What follows are the stories of two antebellum governors who made headlines during their time in Springfield for their crooked and colorful ways.

JOEL MATTESON AND THE GREAT CANAL SCRIP SCANDAL

Joel Aldrich Matteson, Illinois' tenth governor, had the Midas touch. Every business venture he undertook turned to gold. Born of humble origins, by the time he finished his gubernatorial term he was one of the wealthiest men in the state. He lived in what was arguably the biggest and most ornate mansion in Illinois and was rumored to be worth more than $1 million. For all intents and purposes, he was on top of the world. But Matteson was hiding a shocking secret: as governor, he had embezzled more than $200,000 of state fundss

Matteson's lifelong knack for making money made him an unlikely candidate for white-collar crime. When he moved to Illinois from New York as a young man in 1833, Matteson stuffed his wagon full of boots and shoes of all sizes and sold or traded them along the way. He arrived at his destination with more money than when he had started. From then on his fortune only grew. Money made from successful land speculation was reinvested into railroad iron from a defunct rail line, which he promptly shipped to Michigan and sold at a profit. Within a decade of his arrival in Illinois, Matteson's private empire had grown to include a woolen mill, a store, a bank, seven children, the largest home in Joliet and a seat in the Illinois Senate.

When the time came for Democrats to nominate a candidate for governor in 1852, Matteson was the obvious choice. He had ten years' experience as a state senator and had served as chairman of the Senate revenue committee. His business acumen was also much in demand at a time when Illinois was saddled with massive debts from ill-advised loans made under previous administrations. Moreover, this charming, fun-loving man was personally popular. He was elected on November 2, handily defeating Whig candidate Edwin B. Webb (a friend of Lincoln's).

When Matteson, his wife and their seven lovely children swept into Springfield, they became immediate favorites on the social scene—who doesn't like rich people who love to throw parties? The Mattesons, for their part, enjoyed Springfield, with its glittering circle of politicians and businessmen. The only drawback was the official governor's residence, a creaky old two-story structure with practically no yard that used to house the Illinois Board of Public Works. Matteson wanted space to throw parties, and the children wanted more space to play. This house was cramping their style.

To remedy the situation, Matteson persuaded the state auditor and state treasurer that Springfield needed to build an Executive Mansion, and not

Left: Joel Matteson, Illinois' tenth governor, defrauded the state of nearly $250,000. *Courtesy of Portrait and Biographical Album of Jo Daviess and Carroll Counties, Illinois, 1889.*

Below: Not content with the previous official governor's residence, Joel Matteson had this Executive Mansion constructed at a cost of $50,000. *Courtesy of* Springfield, Illinois Illustrated, *1889.*

just any Executive Mansion—a showplace, the largest and most ornate in the West. Several months and $50,000 later ($10,000 of which Matteson advanced from his own pocket), Matteson got his wish. The big brick behemoth topped with its jaunty white cupola was one of the grandest dwellings in the entire state. Nearly one thousand members of the city's elite were invited to the Mattesons' housewarming party on January 10, 1856, which the *Illinois State Register* called "the gayest assemblage ever marshaled in our city" and which even the Republican *Illinois State Journal* conceded was "got up in a style of great magnificence."

Matteson was just getting warmed up. No sooner was the paint dry on the Executive Mansion than he decided that the building was dull and unfashionable and set about building himself a new house directly across the street. Constitutionally limited to one term as governor and smitten with Springfield, Matteson would need someplace to live once his successor took office, and he was determined that his new home should outshine his old one. In this endeavor he was successful. The sprawling Italianate monstrosity he constructed to the tune of $100,000 featured drawing rooms done in oil frescoes, a large library fitted with built-in bookcases and elaborately carved rosewood and mahogany furniture in each of the fourteen bedrooms. The three-acre estate included a double barn, a gardener's cottage, a conservatory, a grape arbor and a sunken garden. If the Executive Mansion was extravagant, the Matteson mansion was downright ostentatious. Joel Matteson couldn't be more pleased. It was just the type of residence that befitted a rich, popular former governor.

If Matteson had had his druthers, it would have been the residence of a rich, popular sitting Democratic United States senator. During the 1855 senatorial election, while he was still the sitting governor, he had allowed his name to be put forward in nomination and, with only a few bribes to grease the wheels, came within a hair of being elected. Only Abraham Lincoln's last-minute sacrifice of his own senatorial hopes thwarted Matteson's plans.

The candidates that year were sharply divided over the issue of the Kansas-Nebraska Act, which effectively repealed the Missouri Compromise of 1820 and opened the western territories to the possibility of slavery. Abraham Lincoln, the Whig candidate, strongly opposed it, as did Democratic candidate Lyman Trumbull. James Shields, another Democratic candidate, strongly favored it. The Democrats felt that it was imperative they elect a "Nebraska man" but also felt that Shields would not be able to muster up enough support to claim victory. Seeing his chance, Matteson shrewdly persuaded them to dump Shields and rally behind him as soon as it became

Not long after the Executive Mansion (right) was completed, Joel Matteson built a larger, grander private residence for himself directly across the street (left). *Courtesy of Sangamon Valley Collection, Lincoln Library, Springfield, Illinois.*

clear that Shields could not win. After all, Matteson pointed out, he had appeal to both Nebraska and anti-Nebraska Democrats.

In those days, senators were elected in a joint session of the state General Assembly rather than by popular vote. Whoever received fifty votes won the seat. When the first ballot was counted, Lincoln led by forty-five votes, Shields had forty, Trumbull had five and Matteson had a single vote. Things continued in largely the same vein through five more ballots, but on the sixth ballot, Matteson started to pick up steam. By the ninth ballot he had forty-seven votes, just three shy of victory; Trumbull had thirty-five, and Lincoln was down to only fifteen. Lincoln saw the writing on the wall and threw his votes to Trumbull on the tenth ballot to prevent Matteson from winning, and Trumbull was elected senator. Mary Lincoln was furious at Trumbull, who she believed had selfishly stolen the election from her husband, and from that day forward she refused to speak to Trumbull's wife, Julia, who had been a bridesmaid in her wedding. Lincoln, for his part, regretted his defeat but, with an uncharacteristic flash of schadenfreude, later remarked that Matteson's "defeat gives me more pleasure than my own gives me pain."

Matteson probably wasn't fit to hold the office of senator, anyway, given his proclivities for defrauding the state. Two years after leaving office, he was implicated in what came to be called the Great Canal Scrip Scandal, which had lined his pockets with better than $200,000.

Back in 1839, the largely bankrupt state of Illinois had issued $338,554 of scrip in fifty- and one-hundred-dollar denominations to help fund the

Matteson fraudulently redeemed a trunk full of uncanceled canal scrip. *Courtesy of Illinois State Archives.*

construction of the Illinois & Michigan Canal. Over the next few years, all except $316 was redeemed. The state's financial recordkeeping being the sloppy mess that it was, however, not all the scrip was cancelled when it was redeemed, nor was the name of the redeemer noted. Instead, much of it found its way back to the canal offices in Chicago, where it sat forgotten for the better part of a decade.

Governor Matteson stumbled across the redeemed but uncancelled scrip in Chicago soon after taking office in 1853 and apparently decided that it would be safer in his custody than in the canal offices. He ordered the clerk to pack the canal records and scrip into a trunk and send it to the governor's office in Springfield.

There the trunk sat for three years, innocently enough, full of all those blank checks that nobody in the world knew about. But Matteson's forbearance had its limits; there was only so long that he could live with the temptation of a trunk full of free money in his basement. In 1856, he started redeeming the scrip, trading it in for state bonds that he deposited, conveniently enough, into banks that he owned.

He nearly got away with it. It wasn't until three years after he left office that a shrewd state congressman caught wind of fraudulent scrip in circulation and looked into the matter. He discovered that Matteson had redeemed almost $250,000 worth of scrip on the sly. An official investigation was convened, and Matteson's guilt quickly became apparent. "It is clear beyond doubt that he stole them," the Illinois secretary of state wrote in his diary.

Unable to come up with a clever alibi for redeeming cancelled scrip, Matteson offered a stupid one: he claimed that he bought the scrip in good faith without realizing that it was no good. From whom? He didn't know. What were their names? He couldn't remember. But it wasn't his fault; he had "unconsciously and innocently been made the instrument through which a gross fraud upon the people has been attempted," as he wrote in a letter to the investigating committee. Then, fearful of his reputation and eager to avoid arrest, he offered to repay the state for the scrip he hadn't stolen and chalk it up to an honest mistake.

The state's high-ranking Republicans were not about to let him off the hook that quickly. They had a bona fide Democratic embezzler on their hands, and they wanted to make an example of him. Already the Republican press had taken to calling Matteson's home, which had quickly morphed into a monument to corruption and greed, "Scrip Villa." They wanted to see the Scrip Villain brought down.

However, Matteson was slippery, and he had friends in high places. His lawyers initially tried to shift the blame to a former canal trustee who happened to be dead, no doubt figuring the late Joseph B. Wells wouldn't

Matteson's private residence became a metaphor for greed and corruption during the Great Canal Scrip Scandal. *Courtesy of Sangamon Valley Collection, Lincoln Library, Springfield, Illinois.*

mind taking the fall. When that didn't work, and a jury was called to decide if Matteson should be indicted for larceny and made to stand trial, rumors flew that it was packed with Matteson cronies rather than with the regular court panel. In the end, his underhanded machinations worked, and he was let off without a trial. Instead, he mortgaged his property and repaid the state $200,000 of the $225,000 that he owed for money he claimed he hadn't stolen.

All did not end well for Matteson, however. Although he was never formally charged with a crime, he was informally charged with being a crooked bastard, and this charge happened to stick. To escape the sting of public disfavor, Matteson packed up his family and went to Europe for two years to lay low and let the scandal blow over.

Things did not improve much for him upon his return. The Civil War had hit his business interests hard, and his banks were hemorrhaging money. Eventually, his mansion was sold at auction for $40,000—less than half of what it had cost him to build—though it was purchased by his son-in-law, who allowed him to continue living there. But no kindly son-in-law could save the mansion from being engulfed in flames on January 28, 1873, after a careless caretaker left a fire untended while he went home to dinner. Matteson, already in poor health from being thrown from a buggy several weeks earlier, reportedly could not stand the shock of losing his beloved home. He died three days later, on January 31.

WILLIAM H. BISSELL'S DUEL, DISINGENUOUSNESS AND DEBILITATING DISEASE

As Illinois governors go, William H. Bissell was not a bad guy. By all accounts he was pleasant and likeable—a modest, reticent man with a sharp wit who wrote beautifully and spoke powerfully for the cause of his party and his country. Over the course of his life he held many careers: doctor, lawyer, soldier, congressman, governor—all of which he performed ably. As a statesman, he was passionately devoted to the Union and always tried to act in its defense. Still, quite unintentionally, Bissell often found himself at the center of controversies and scandals, making him one of the most colorful characters to have served as governor of Illinois.

He came to Illinois from New York in the 1830s, when he was in his mid-twenties, and set himself up as a doctor. He held a degree from Philadelphia

Illinois's eleventh governor, William H. Bissell, perjured himself while taking the oath of office when he swore that he'd never been challenged to a duel. *Courtesy of Portrait & Biographical Album of Jo Daviess and Carroll Counties, Illinois, 1889.*

Medical College, though it must be remembered that early nineteenth-century medical degrees could be obtained in a matter of months and were largely considered optional. He quickly made friends in Illinois and by 1840 had been elected to serve in the state legislature on the Democratic ticket. His stint in the statehouse gave him a taste for politics and the law, so he abandoned medicine and became a lawyer.

In 1846, war broke out with Mexico, and President Polk put out a call for volunteers to fight. Bissell was one of the first to enlist and was soon elected colonel of the mostly Democratic Second Illinois Regiment. He quickly found that military life was not all that it was cracked up to be: mile after mile of marching through the hot, dusty Mexican desert; intense boredom; homesickness; and poor rations. It would seem that there were only two bright spots of military life, as far as Bissell was concerned: the comradeship of his fellow soldiers and the Mexican ladies.

In February 1847, more than six months after enlisting, he finally had his chance for glory in the Battle of Buena Vista, when the Second Kentucky, First Illinois and Bissell's Second Illinois regiments held the line under some of the most intense fighting of the entire war. Bissell returned to Illinois a hero. He brought with him from Mexico a reputation that paved the way for his eventual political triumphs. Little did he know that he also brought home a disease that would cripple him and contribute to his early death.

The disease would not manifest itself for several more years, but the reputation as a war hero paid off almost immediately. A year after his return to Illinois, Bissell was sent to Congress, borne aloft by a rush of popular acclaim. He arrived right in the middle of the bitterest sectional conflict the nation had ever seen. The United States, in its victory over Mexico, had acquired a vast section of territory, encompassing present-day California, Nevada, Utah and parts of Arizona, Colorado and New Mexico. The

William H. Bissell led the Second Illinois Regiment to glory in the Battle of Buena Vista during the Mexican-American War. *Courtesy of John Frost's* Pictorial History of Mexico and the Mexican War, *1849.*

question of how and where slavery should be allowed in this new land stirred up a maelstrom of controversy. Southerners wanted slavery in as much of the territory as possible; after all, these territories would one day become states, and these states would send representatives to Congress. Northerners would have preferred to keep slavery out of the territory altogether.

Bissell, from his seat in the House of Representatives, listened with growing disgust to what he called the "insolent, overbearing and bullying" southern congressmen as they pressed their case and threatened disunion. He was especially annoyed by the wily, cadaverous Representative from Virginia, James Seddon, who, high on southern pride but low on facts, credited the Mississippi regiment with saving the day at the Battle of Buena Vista. Finally, Bissell felt compelled to speak up—not because he was seeking the spotlight, he later explained, but "because nobody else seemed inclined to do aught except to sit and cower under the lash of these damned negro drivers." On February 21, 1850, he stood and delivered a speech that essentially told the South where it could stuff it and wound up by retorting that the Mississippi regiment was "not within a mile and a half of the scene of action" at Buena Vista—that distinction belonged to the regiments from Illinois and Kentucky, and any claim to the contrary was "a cruel injustice" upon the men who had fought and died that day.

The speech was a tremendous success. Eighty thousand copies were printed for distribution. Notes of congratulations and support poured in from across the country. Bissell skyrocketed to national fame. The North loved him. The South wanted to kill him.

One southerner in particular took it upon himself to try.

Jefferson Davis, senator from Mississippi and future president of the Confederacy, hadn't actually been present to hear Bissell's speech. He probably hadn't even read it. But he had heard enough about it to know that Bissell had not only scorned his beloved Dixie but had also insulted the Mississippi regiment that Davis had commanded in the Mexican War. For that, Davis decided, he must die. He sent a note to Bissell asking for an explanation of what was said in the speech, and when the reply he received was not to his liking, he sent another note challenging Bissell to a duel. Bissell, never one to shrink from a fight, accepted and suggested army muskets loaded with buckshot from a distance of ten paces. Bissell's choice of weapons indicated that he meant business: muskets packed considerably more firepower than standard dueling pistols, and at ten paces they would blow a man to pieces.

Jefferson Davis challenged William H. Bissell to a duel over a perceived slight to the Mississippi regiment he commanded during the Battle of Buena Vista. *Courtesy of Library of Congress, Prints and Photographs Division.*

Luckily for Bissell, Davis and the Confederacy, the duel never happened. Somewhere along the line Bissell was persuaded to modify his statement regarding the Battle of Buena Vista, taking extra pains to praise the gallantry of the Mississippi regiment. Some have suggested that President Zachary Taylor, Bissell's commander in the Mexican War and Davis's former father-in-law, intervened to prevent bloodshed. Whatever the case, both men survived to fulfill their destinies: Davis to become president of the Confederate States of America, Bissell to become governor of Illinois.

In fact, the gravest threat to Bissell's life was not posed by an angry southerner wielding a musket but by the insidious bacteria that his body had been harboring for years. It struck with full force the winter of 1851, leaving him almost completely paralyzed from the waist down. The illness would wax and wane over the next few years. By 1852, he was forced to do his campaigning for Congress seated in a chair or carriage. By 1854, he declined to run at all.

No one was exactly sure what Bissell was suffering from. Some believed that an unfortunate bout with chronic diarrhea while in Mexico was to blame. Less credibly, others suggested that a childhood injury to his spine had inexplicably now flared up or that he had injured himself when jumping off a train. His malady was called, variously, "partial paralysis," "neuralgia" or simply the "mysterious disease."

If anyone guessed the real culprit, they were polite enough not to mention it publicly; in all likelihood Bissell had contracted syphilis in Mexico. It was common for soldiers, lonely and far from home, to seek comfort with prostitutes or keep a "señorita" in their quarters. Saltillo, where his regiment was posted before and after the Battle of Buena Vista, was a hotbed of venereal diseases; people later speculated that infected prostitutes there had done more harm to U.S. troops than Santa Anna's army. Syphilis was a particularly nasty disease. After an initial flare-up, it could remain latent for many years, as it probably had done with Bissell. Now, however, the disease was awake and hungry, and Bissell's pelvic bone was being slowly and painfully devoured by this vicious Mexican souvenir. For the rest of his life he would need crutches to get around.

Ill as he was, he consented to run for governor of Illinois in 1856 under the banner of the newly formed Republican Party. Abraham Lincoln's name had initially been floated as a candidate, but Lincoln demurred, believing that only a former Democrat who opposed the contentious Kansas-Nebraska Act would have a chance of winning. Bissell was the logical choice: he had been an anti-Nebraska Democrat, he was a war hero and he was popular. He was almost the perfect candidate. Almost.

The one tiny drawback to Bissell's candidacy was, ironically, part of the reason he was so popular to begin with: the little matter of the challenge to duel issued by Jefferson Davis that he had accepted five years earlier. According to the 1848 Illinois Constitution, anyone who had ever given or accepted a challenge to duel was barred from holding state office. Should Bissell be elected, he would have to swear an oath that he had never been involved in a duel.

Obviously this was something that he could not quite honestly do. The Democrats were only too happy to bring this fact to public attention, warning that Bissell could not assume office without perjuring himself by taking the oath.

Strictly speaking, they were correct, but Bissell and his fellow Republicans were not about to give up the governor's seat over a small hiccup like perjury. Instead, they came up with a rather disingenuous rationalization for Bissell's continued candidacy: the challenge to duel had been accepted in Washington, D.C., not Illinois, and was therefore not subject to the dictates of the Illinois Constitution. It was slippery, but it worked: Bissell was elected with a plurality of almost five thousand votes and blithely took the oath of office the following January. Although it is unclear how Bissell felt about his equivocation, some of his friends later suggested that torment over his perceived wrongdoing helped drive him to his early grave.

His term of service was not without missteps. The most embarrassing of these blunders took place barely a month after he assumed office and required Lincoln's help to sort out.

On February 18, 1857, Bissell was handed a stack of 149 bills to look over. Although he had an office in the statehouse, his disability prevented him from using it, and he worked most days from an office in the Executive Mansion. Among the papers that his secretary dropped off were an apportionment bill and an appropriation bill. He meant to veto the former and sign the latter.

Instead, he mistakenly signed the apportionment bill (which disgusted Republicans called "An Act to Violate the Constitution, and Disenfranchise the People of this State"), putting his stamp of approval on a Democratic plan to gerrymander the state's election districts and thereby disenfranchise countless members of his own Republican Party. The Democratically controlled General Assembly shouted and cheered when the news came that Bissell had signed the bill.

Their joy was short lived. A half hour later another message arrived, this time stating that Bissell had signed the bill by mistake and was now vetoing it. Now it was the Republicans' turn to cheer, while the Democrats got up and stalked out in disgust, refusing to recognize the veto. As far as they were concerned, there were no take-backs—once Bissell put his name on that bill, it became law.

The matter was eventually settled in the Illinois Supreme Court early in 1858. The Democratic plaintiffs challenged the validity of the veto, but the defense, led by Lincoln, was successful in arguing that the governor had every right to strike his signature and replace it with a veto while the bill was still in his control.

Lincoln had a personal stake in seeing Bissell's veto upheld: he was contemplating a run for the Senate later that year. Because senators in those days were elected by members of the state General Assembly and not by popular vote, it was in his own interest to see that a bill creating more Democratic districts was not passed. Of course, he lost the Senate seat to Stephen A. Douglas but won a national reputation that sent him to the White House two years later.

Bissell did not live to see Lincoln's presidential victory. After years of steady decline, he caught pneumonia and died on March 18, 1860 at age forty-eight. He was the first Illinois governor to die in office.

Chapter 3

SEX, SLANDER AND FIGHTING

They say that seldom does the course of love run smoothly. As an attorney who handled dozens of divorce cases throughout his career, Abraham Lincoln witnessed firsthand the range of misdeeds that drove couples apart. Some were quietly heartbreaking, such as the husbands who went off to California during the gold rush and were never heard from again or the wives who went to visit their relatives and didn't come back. Some were horrific, such as the husbands who habitually got drunk and beat their wives and children. And many were downright salacious. We might think of our nineteenth-century forbears as prim and proper, but the court records tell a different story: people in Lincoln's time evidently liked sex as much as anyone—and not always necessarily with their spouses.

They also liked to talk. Tidbits of information passed back and forth across backyard fences, in the shops and saloons, at dinner parties and at church. And in Lincoln's Springfield, a man's reputation could be made or broken based on what people were saying about him. It was an era when a man's good name counted for a lot. Before credit checks and registered sex offender lists, a man's ability to do business, obtain credit and gain acceptance in society was based solely on his reputation for honesty and integrity. In a world where paper money was scarce and most purchases were done on credit, any hint of scandal or shady dealings could make it difficult for him to buy anything from land to groceries. Consequently, men went out of their way to protect their reputations, often by suing their maligners for slander. It is a testament to the value of a man's reputation

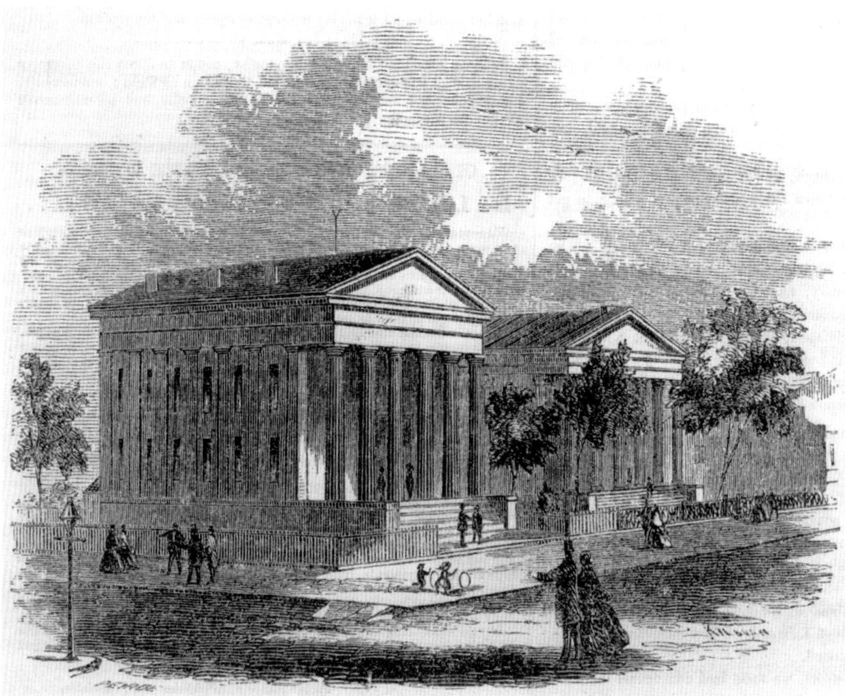

Springfield's divorce, slander and assault cases were pled before the Sangamon County Circuit Court (left). *Courtesy of* Ballou's Pictorial Drawing-Room Companion, *1856.*

in antebellum America that an Illinois statute allowed damages of up to $1,000 in slander suits.

Women were careful of their reputations, as well. The best things a woman had going for her were her sexual purity before marriage and her fidelity after marriage. Loss of either of these virtues would make it exceedingly difficult to catch or keep a husband. Even the suggestion of sexual impropriety was enough to stain a woman in society's eyes. While women weren't generally given to dueling, they did defend their reputations in court with slander suits; lacking legal rights of their own, they had to file jointly with their husbands.

Just as a man's good name counted for a lot in Lincoln's time, so did a man's honor, especially among men who had been born in the South. More than just the way the community perceived a man, the concept of honor also included how a man saw himself. An honorable man was strong and courageous, honest and direct and able to provide for his family. A dishonorable man was worthy of self-contempt and social ostracization. In antebellum Springfield, an affront to a man's honor was often paid for with blood. Upper-class men issued challenges to duel, as James Shields did when he believed himself to have been insulted by Abraham Lincoln (more on that later). Common folk, on the other hand, fought with their fists. And fighting on the frontier was nasty.

The stories that follow show the seedy side of Springfield's inhabitants: the unsavory sexual peccadilloes, gossip malicious enough to be considered slander and a fistfight that left one combatant in danger of losing an eye.

LOVERS, BROTHELS AND VENEREAL DISEASES

James Brown's marriage went bad sometime about 1840. He didn't want to believe it at first. He and Maria had been married since 1830 and for several years had been so happy together. He'd done everything in his power to see that she was well taken care of, he treated her with respect and affection and he'd bought her every luxury he could afford.

Then they moved to Springfield in 1838, and things started to change. Maria made a lot of friends, mostly men. She spent more and more time with them. People started to talk. James grew uneasy but chose to believe the best of his wife and assumed that nothing untoward was going on. Still, he begged her to be more circumspect with her friendships with these men and to take into consideration the talk she was stirring up and the hurt she was causing him.

Maria, however, wasn't about to let her husband's nagging get in the way of a good time. She started inviting men over to their room in the boardinghouse while James was out, entertaining them behind closed doors and without a chaperone. One man in particular caught her eye: the hotblooded Dr. Elias H. Merryman, captain of the Springfield Artillery Company. He was handsome and attentive—and he made house calls.

Poor, thick James still wasn't catching on, not even when their landlord, citing Maria's scandalous behavior, kicked them out of the boardinghouse and insisted they find new lodgings. He still hung on to the hope that her behavior, if imprudent, was not licentious, though he begged her again to think about how her behavior was affecting her reputation in town. He even wrote her a letter to this effect when he was away on business, pleading hurt feelings and raising the specter of social disgrace.

Maria was starting to lose patience with her killjoy husband. She showed the letter to Merryman, and they both had a good laugh over it. By this time she and James were living at a new boardinghouse, and Merryman had taken to spending the night during James's frequent absences from home. It did not escape the notice of the new landlords that Maria was having sleepovers with the doctor, and soon enough the Browns were kicked out of this boardinghouse, too.

Finally, James started to suspect that something might be amiss in his marriage. Talking to Maria wasn't getting him anywhere; if anything, she was only growing more shameless. Meanwhile, the town gossips were having a field day with Maria's scandalous behavior and James's laughable ignorance. On September 26, 1840, however, James came face to face with evidence of his wife's infidelity that he couldn't ignore: he found a love letter in her handwriting to Elias Merryman hidden under a flowerpot on the windowsill of their room.

Slowly, James put two and two together: a love letter from his wife to Dr. Merryman; the constant visits he made to Maria when James was away; getting kicked out of two boardinghouses on account of Maria's indecent behavior; and the rumors swirling around town. Why, Maria must be having an affair with Elias Merryman!

Wounded, James confronted Maria with the letter and stormed out of the house. Imagine his dismay when he walked by later and found yet another letter to Merryman sitting under the flowerpot. James could no longer escape the fact that his marriage was over. In the summer of 1841, he filed for divorce, pouring out his entire sad story to his attorney Stephen T. Logan, who, with help from his partner Abraham Lincoln, wrote up the bill for divorce. In July, the Sangamon County Circuit Court granted the divorce, but only James was there to witness the dissolution of their union. Displaying the same interest in her divorce that she had in her marriage, Maria Brown had failed to show up in court.

James Brown wasn't the only person in Springfield with a philandering spouse on his hands. Cynthia Klein was certain that her husband had spent time in every house of ill fame in Springfield. She might have been willing to overlook this offensive behavior if he hadn't also been an alcoholic who liked to use his fists on her when he was drunk, which was most of the time. She tolerated the beatings for several years, but when he threatened to shoot her, she feared he just might make good on his threat. Deciding that enough was enough, she moved out of the house. In September 1859, she hired Abraham Lincoln and William H. Herndon as her attorneys

The law office of Lincoln & Herndon. *Courtesy of* Frank Leslie's Illustrated Newspaper, *December 22, 1860.*

and filed for divorce, charging John with cruelly "whipping—beating—and bruising" her and citing in particular one instance where only the intervention of some passersby kept him from choking her to death. Given John's fondness for the bottle and terrible temper, she was seeking freedom from the man who made her fear for her life.

John was only too happy to agree to a divorce, but he wanted the record set straight. He categorically denied being a habitual drunkard. Furthermore, he denied ever beating his wife or threatening to kill her. And while he admitted it was true that he had been to every whorehouse in town, he had only done that after Cynthia had left him.

In fact, he went on to charge, Cynthia was the one with loose morals. He brought in a witness who testified that he had frequently heard Cynthia screaming and cursing at her husband. Furthermore, he had seen Cynthia keeping company with Nancy Doolittle, the madam of one of the town's brothels. John's ace up his sleeve, however, was the family's domestic servant, Anna Stacy Freeman. According to her testimony, Cynthia had struck her husband more than once while in a fit of rage. Cynthia was also in the habit of drinking liquor—the servant had seen her drunk. Finally, not only was Cynthia friends with Nancy Doolittle, but she had also invited the madam over while John was away, and the two women had a grand old time drinking and carousing, even though Cynthia's impressionable young children were around.

Cynthia Klein would long rue the day she had run afoul of her hired girl. In light of Anna's damning testimony, Cynthia's petition for a divorce was denied. Instead, the court granted John the divorce—and because

Cynthia's "abandoned character and corrupt associates" would be "ruinous to the morals" of the children, John was granted full custody of the children, as well.

Sarah Kyle thought that her husband was not only ruinous to the morals of her children, but he was also ruinous to her health. Thanks to him, she was now the unhappy carrier of a venereal disease. In March 1846, she filed for divorce, charging him with adultery. Just so everyone was clear, she spelled out the cause of her suspicion in the bill for divorce: Joseph Kyle had infected her with a disease that he must have picked up from another woman.

Her husband hired Abraham Lincoln as his attorney and tried to defend himself against the unsavory accusation. In what can only have been an uncomfortable interview between lawyer and client, Lincoln listened as Joseph told his side of the story. It was true that he had become infected with a disease about 1839, and he supposed if you were to press him on it he would have to admit that, yes, it was a venereal disease, and he guessed he might have passed said venereal disease on to his wife. Still, he swore that he was not infected through illicit sexual intercourse. He had explained as much to Sarah in 1839, telling her that he must have caught the disease in a Springfield outhouse. Sarah had continued living and sleeping with him anyway, thus making her the only woman in the history of the world who has bought the "caught it from an outhouse" excuse for a sexually transmitted disease.

She wouldn't buy it forever, though. In late 1845, Joseph had another flare-up of the disease. Sarah got suspicious. Joseph got defensive. He suggested that perhaps *he* had caught it from *her*. But in retrospect, it might not have been a venereal disease this time, because it cleared up quickly, without even a visit to the doctor. Anyway, he concluded to Lincoln, he couldn't have caught the disease in late 1845 because he had been laid up at home with illness most of the time. He had hardly left the neighborhood, and there were no prostitutes in the neighborhood; ergo, he could not have had any illicit intercourse.

Lincoln, from whose pen would one day flow such masterpieces of prose as the Gettysburg Address and the Second Inaugural, dutifully wrote up a court document describing his client's explanation of the outhouse and venereal disease. He submitted it to the court in answer to the bill for divorce, hoping to halt the proceedings.

It was all for naught. The court found in favor of the plaintiff and granted Sarah Kyle a divorce, as well as full custody of the couple's two

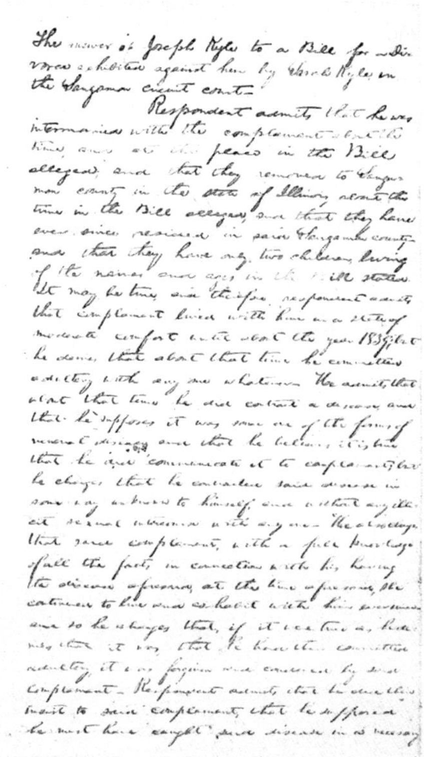

The answer of Joseph Kyle to a Bill for a Divorce exhibited against him by Sarah Kyle in the Sangamon circuit court—

Respondent admits that he was intermarried with the complainant about the time and at the place in the Bill alleged; and that they removed to Sangamon county in the State of Illinois about the time in the Bill alleged; and that they have ever since resided in said Sangamon county; and that they have only two children living of the names and ages in the Bill stated. It may be true and therefore respondent admits that complainant lived with him in a state of moderate comfort until about the year 1839, but he denies that about that time he committed adultery with any one whatever. He admits that about that time he did contract a disease and that he supposes it was some one of the forms of venereal disease; and that he believes it is true that he did communicate it to complainant; but he charges that he contracted said disease in some way unknown to himself, and without any illicit sexual intercourse with any one. He also charges that said complainant, with a full knowledge of all the facts, in connection with his having the disease aforesaid, at the time aforesaid, she continued to live and cohabit with him ever since; and so he charges that, if it be true, as he denies that it was, that he has then committed adultery it was forgiven and condoned by said complainant— Respondent admits that he did tell this much to said complainant, that he supposed he must have caught said disease in a necessary

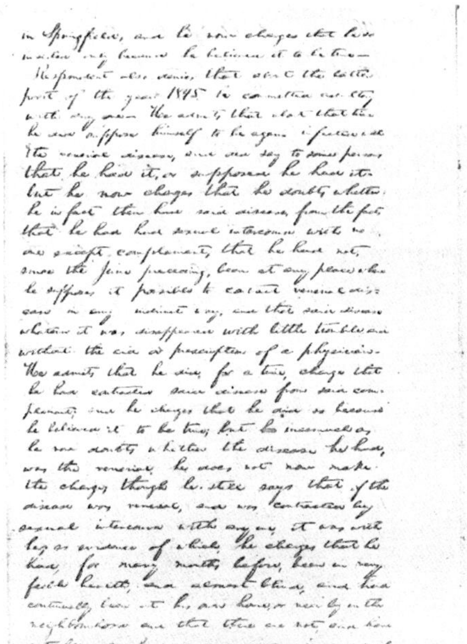

in Springfield, and he now charges that his mention was because he believed it to be true—

Respondent also denies, that about the latter part of the year 1845 he committed adultery with any one. He admits that about that time he did suppose himself to be again infected with the venereal disease, and did say to some persons that he had it, or supposed he had it—but he now charges that he doubts whether he in fact then had said disease, from the fact that he had had sexual intercourse with no one except complainant; that he had not, since the time preceding, been at any place where he supposes it possible to catch venereal disease in any indirect way, and that said disease whatever it was, disappeared with little trouble and without the aid or prescription of a physician. He admits that he did, for a time, charge that he had contracted said disease from said complainant; and he charges that he did so because he believed it to be true; but inasmuch as he now doubts whether the disease he had, was the venereal, he does not now make the charge; though he still says that if the disease was venereal, and was contracted by sexual intercourse with any one it was with her as evidence of which, he charges that she had, for many months before, been in very feeble health, and almost blind, and had continually been at his own house or near by in the neighborhood and that there are not, and have not been, any lewd or common women in said neighborhood, from whom he could have contracted such a disease. Respondent denies all the other

matters charged in said Bill, and he denies that if they were true, they would constitute a cause of divorce— He also denies the right of said complainant to the custody of said children, or to alimony against him—

And now having fully answered he prays, to be hence dismissed with his reasonable costs—

Lincoln & Herndon p.d.

Lincoln wrote this legal document on behalf of Joseph Kyle, who tried to suggest that he had caught his veneral disease from an outhouse. *Courtesy of Library of Congress, Herndon-Weik Collection.*

children. Sarah was free of her diseased husband (though not free of the disease), Joseph was free to fornicate with prostitutes to his heart's desire and Lincoln was free to turn his talent for writing to slightly more inspiring topics.

SLANDEROUS STATEMENTS AND ATROCIOUS ACCUSATIONS

Martha Beatty, wife of William Beatty, woke up one morning in May 1845 to find her reputation hanging by a thread, thanks to the neighborhood grapevine. Old Tom Vandegrist had gotten to flapping his jaws with John Miller at the tanning yard and started saying nasty things about Martha, things that could ruin a woman's good standing in the community. He said that he had heard Martha was caught having sex with Dr. Sullivan in the Beattys' stable early one morning.

John Miller, titillated by this little piece of gossip, went home and repeated it to his wife. Susan Miller, who couldn't be expected to keep this juicy nugget to herself, repeated it to a few more people. "Mrs. Beatty and Dr. Sullivan were seen together in Beatty's stable, one morning, very early, in the very act. They were caught in the very act!"

This sleazy rumor got back to the Beattys, and they were incensed. It really wouldn't do to have the community thinking that Mrs. Beatty was being unchaste in her very own stable, all because Susan Miller liked to gossip. They were so incensed, in fact, that they hired silver-tongued, English-born sitting congressman Edward D. Baker as their attorney and filed a slander suit against John and Susan Miller. (At that time, Mary Lincoln happened to be pregnant with her second son, who would be named Edward Baker Lincoln in Baker's honor.)

The Millers hired the firm of Lincoln & Herndon to defend them and pleaded not guilty. Susan maintained that her statements weren't slanderous—they were the truth. "It is certainly a fact," she insisted. "Jo Shepherd can prove it by two respectable witnesses." When pressed on the matter, though, the Millers declaimed all intention of trying to prove the rumor they had helped spread.

It is an ironic fact of a slander case that, to clear one's good name, one must forbear having the offending rumor repeated to the jury during trial, but that's exactly the indignity Martha Beatty had to undergo. By the

Martha Beatty hired Congressman Edward D. Baker to file a slander suit against John and Susan Miller. *Courtesy of Library of Congress, Prints and Photographs Division.*

end of the day, every single person in the crowded courtroom knew that there was a story (true or not) that she had been caught in the act with her doctor in the stable.

On the bright side, John and Susan Miller were found guilty of slander and forced to pay William and Martha Beatty forty-five dollars in damages. One can only hope that this sum was worth the mortification Martha suffered in the whole affair.

Two years later, over in Christian County, Illinois, William Torrence also found himself the victim of slanderous talk. Only this talk didn't just leave him mortified. It left him humiliated.

Newton Galloway had accused him, in front of a big group of his friends and neighbors, of "the infamous crime against nature with a beast."

Galloway hadn't used those exact words, of course. What he had said was that Torrence "caught my old sow and fucked her as long as he could." And that wasn't all. He went on to say, in front of all those people, that Torrence "knocked up my old sow and is now bellying down and will soon have some young bills."

While this might not have been the same kind of defamation of character that would make it hard for him to get credit at the corner store, it nevertheless stung. William Torrence wanted vengeance or, barring that, a hefty cash compensation for his suffering.

He retained Herndon & Lincoln and filed a slander suit seeking $1,000 in damages from Newton Galloway for his dirty talk. (One can only imagine the jokes that were later traded in the firm's office over this case.) When the day of the trial arrived, however, Torrence lost his nerve and failed to appear in court, perhaps not having the stomach for hearing a recitation of the slanderous statement in court. Since Galloway also neglected to show, the case was continued to the next term of court.

In June of the following year, Torrence slunk into court and dismissed the case at his cost. History does not record whether he ever saw Galloway—or his sow—again.

As an interesting postscript to this story, in 2005, the town of Taylorville, Illinois, county seat of Christian County, decided to erect a bronze statue of Lincoln in its central square in front of the courthouse. Casting about for an idea more original and less expensive than Lincoln astride a horse, the town finally decided to commemorate an incident from Lincoln's lawyering days before the Christian County Court. Unable to make himself heard over the noise of hogs rooting around under the courthouse, Lincoln asked Judge David Davis to issue a "writ of quietus" to the offending hogs. The result is, as the town proclaims, "the world's only statue of Lincoln with a pig," proudly displayed in the world's only place where a client of Lincoln's was accused of impregnating just such a beast.

FIGHTING DIRTY

The mountains and rivers of Kentucky and Tennessee, where half of antebellum Springfield's residents were born, echo with the stories of legendary fights and the legendary disfigurements they produced. The style of fighting to come out of the backcountry was called "rough and tumble," and there were precious few rules. It was common for brawlers to kick and pull hair and yank testicles; it was not unheard of that a man's ear or lip should be bitten off.

The coup de grâce of frontier fighting, however—the equivalent of a knockout punch—was if one combatant could succeed in gouging the other man's eye out. A man who was traveling through Kentucky in the early nineteenth century described what he called the "frightfully cruel" practice of gouging: "It consisted in allowing the finger-nails to grow so long, that, by cutting them, you could give them the form of a small sickle, and this strange weapon was used, in the broils that constantly occurred, to cut out the eyes of the hostile party." Other accounts detailed the grisly satisfaction that a victorious combatant took in ripping an eye from its socket. In the backwoods South, men without eyes were common sights.

The upland southerners who migrated to Springfield took their practice of vicious fighting with them, and brawls were common occurrences both

James P. Hawthorn did the backbreaking work of clearing thirty-eight acres of sod for David Wooldridge, only to be stiffed of his pay. *Courtesy of Library of Congress, Prints and Photographs Division.*

in and outside of town. James P. Hawthorn learned this firsthand when he had the misfortune to run afoul of David Wooldridge, a thirty-five-year-old Kentucky-born farmer with a violent streak.

Hawthorn was a young, single man working as a tenant farmer on Wooldridge's land. By the spring of 1835 he'd fallen behind on his rent. He now owed Wooldridge in the neighborhood of $300—quite a sum in a time when cash was hard to come by. Wooldridge gave him the opportunity to make some money, offering to pay him $50 for breaking twenty acres of sod. As a bonus, if Hawthorn broke another eighteen acres of sod, Wooldridge would let him use it, rent-free, for as long as it took to grow a crop of wheat or corn.

Hawthorn agreed and sometime within a year succeeded in busting the thirty-eight acres of sod. It was miserable, backbreaking work. Hawthorn would have been tromping through prairie grass that was knee-deep and wet with dew, guiding the iron plow through the hard sod and coaxing two sometimes-uncooperative yoke of cattle forward. His progress would have been halted frequently—sometimes to take an axe to the thick roots known as "devils shoestrings," often times to clean the blade of the plow when the soil clung to it and rendered it useless and occasionally to chase off snakes. Exhausted but triumphant after accomplishing this feat, Hawthorn went to Wooldridge to claim his pay.

To his utter disgust, Wooldridge not only refused to pay him the fifty dollars, but he also refused to let Hawthorn farm the eighteen acres.

One can only imagine the tensions running between the two men when they came face to face to discuss the matter of payment. Wooldridge was almost certainly upset over Hawthorn's failure to pay the rent and felt that he didn't owe his tenant a dime for the work he had just completed. Hawthorn, who hadn't just spent weeks pushing a plow through hard-packed sod for his health, doubtless was enraged at having been stiffed for his labors. He came to the conclusion that Wooldridge had tricked him into performing the unpleasant work, all the while never intending to pay him at all.

On June 5, 1836, the conflict escalated into violence. History does not record who threw the first punch, but Wooldridge clearly got the best of his opponent; he "struck, beat, bruised, and knocked down" Hawthorn and then "plucked, pulled, and tore divers large quantities of hair" from his head. Just getting warmed up, he proceeded to beat Hawthorn with a stick and with his fists. But he wasn't done yet. With Hawthorn writhing in agony on the ground, Wooldridge "violently kicked" him and beat him some more. Finally, Wooldridge finished up by thrusting his "thumbs and fingers into the eyes" of his opponent to "gouge" him, causing him, as Hawthorn put it, "great pain, distress, and injury."

After the fight, Hawthorn was left "hurt, bruised, and wounded." He remained so "sick, sore, wounded and partially blind" for the next six weeks that he was unable to perform any work. Not only did he miss out on the chance to earn wages during the height of the agricultural season, but he also had to dip into his savings to pay for the medical attention his injuries required. Now, he believed, Wooldridge owed him more than ever. Not only had he cheated him out of payment for breaking thirty-eight acres of sod, but he was also now responsible for Hawthorn's lack of earnings and medical expenses.

Suspecting that asking Wooldridge for money would get him nowhere, and painfully aware that trying to beat the money out of him was out of the question, Hawthorn finally turned to the legal system to exact his payment. In late June 1836, he hired Josephus Hewett as his attorney and filed two lawsuits. One was an assumpsit, or debt collection suit, for $100 to recover the money owed to him for his sod-busting efforts. The second was a trespass *vi et armis* ("with force of arms") suit seeking $500 in lost wages and damages from Wooldridge for assaulting him.

Wooldridge responded by hiring his own attorneys. He selected the firm of John T. Stuart and Henry E. Dummer of Springfield. At the time the suit was filed, Stuart had a young Abraham Lincoln studying law in his office. On September 9, 1836, Abraham Lincoln was formally admitted to the bar, and within one month Stuart had put him to work on the two *Hawthorn v. Wooldridge* cases, Lincoln's first ever as a licensed attorney. Though he was representing the defendant, Lincoln might secretly have sympathized with Hawthorn's plight, at least as far as the sod-breaking went. Lincoln was no stranger to the plow himself, having helped his father clear land for his farm in Macon County just five years earlier.

On Wooldridge's behalf, Stuart, Dummer and Lincoln went on the offensive as much as possible for the defendant in a case. First, they tried to use Hawthorn's poverty against him: they filed affidavits (in Lincoln's hand) advising the court that James Hawthorn did not have any real or personal property with which to fund a lawsuit. If they heard the case, Wooldridge's attorneys warned, "the officers of this court will be in danger of losing their costs in said suit unless the said Plaintiff be ruled to give security therefor." The court saw the wisdom of their words and ordered Hawthorn to provide security, which he did in the person of two friends who swore that they would pay for all court costs. Then they requested a set-off in the assumpsit case for the $314 Hawthorn owed Wooldridge in unpaid rent. Finally, in light of the fact that Wooldridge evidently sustained some damage of his own during the scuffle, they also filed a countersuit of trespass *vi et armis*, although this suit was dismissed by Wooldridge and Hawthorn's mutual consent the same term.

After all the pain and indignity Hawthorn suffered at Wooldridge's hands, and after all the time and trouble it took to file two lawsuits and provide security for them both, Hawthorn gained precious little through litigation. The cases were continued to the spring 1837 term of court, at which time the assumpsit case was dismissed, Wooldridge and Hawthorn having reached some kind of agreement. The trespass case was tried in front of a jury, which found in Hawthorn's favor. Instead of the $500 payout he had been seeking, however, he was awarded a paltry $36, a verdict that might have been the jury's way of slapping his hand for being too greedy in the amount he sought for damages.

Over the course of his legal career, Lincoln would see dozens of examples of creative means men found to inflict pain on one another in rough-and-tumble brawls, including twisting noses, beating with two-foot-long clubs, beating with ropes, beating with iron rods and stabbing with knives. When these cases went to court, the defendants were seldom fined more than $100 and were almost never sent to prison, indicating that, in frontier fights, anything goes.

Chapter 4

SLAVERY IN THE EMANCIPATOR'S HOMETOWN

Slavery had been introduced to Illinois in the seventeenth century, when the region was a French territory. By the time France relinquished control of the Illinois Country to England in 1763, following the French and Indian War, the region was home to nine hundred slaves. Although French residents worried that their new landlords would be hostile to slavery, they had nothing to fear; the English were only too happy to legally recognize the institution.

It wasn't until Illinois became part of the Northwest Territory in 1787 that any attempt was made to curb slavery. Article 6 of the Northwest Ordinance declared that "there shall be neither slavery nor involuntary servitude in the said territory, otherwise than in the punishment of crime, whereof the party shall have been duly convicted." Many Illinois settlers, especially those of French descent, greeted this article with dismay. No more slaves? Slavery was part of their culture, and they were reluctant to give it up. They lobbied for the repeal of Article 6, and when this didn't happen, they craftily found ways to sidestep it.

Arthur St. Clair, the first governor of the Northwest Territory, was the first to create a loophole in the article when he decided in 1790 that it could not be interpreted retroactively. That is to say, anyone who was a slave before the Northwest Ordinance was passed would remain a slave. In a tiny nod to the spirit of the original article, St. Clair did acknowledge that no slaves should be imported into the Northwest Territory from slaveholding states.

This presented a problem for slaveholders. Keeping their old slaves was great, but what if they wanted to buy new slaves? In 1802, William Henry Harrison, governor of the Territory of Indiana and future president of the United States, came up with a potential solution: he called for a ten-year suspension of Article 6 during which slaves could be introduced into the territories, to remain slaves for life. He didn't get very far with that proposition, but he did manage to introduce "A Law Concerning Servants" to the Indiana Territory, which at that time included the Illinois Country. This law spelled out a system of "voluntary" servitude, whereby a slave brought into the territory would be taken to the Court of Common Pleas within thirty days and given a choice of entering into a contract of indentured servitude or being sent back south in chains. When the Illinois Territory was organized in 1809, it was quick to pass its very own indentured servitude law.

Illinois became a state in 1818. For a so-called free state, its constitution was remarkably lax on the issue of slavery, stating that neither slavery nor indentured servitude should "hereafter" be introduced. This was bad news for those already held in bondage. It wasn't great news for indentured servants, either; the constitution fully recognized indentured servitude. Moreover, children born to African American indentured servants would not become free until age eighteen for females and age twenty-one for males.

Free African Americans in Illinois were hardly better off, thanks to the "black laws" borrowed from Kentucky and Virginia and passed by the state legislature in 1819. They decreed that free African Americans were required to have a court-sanctioned certificate of freedom in hand before moving to Illinois. Without this document in hand, any unfortunate soul would be in danger of being arrested, imprisoned and sold into slavery for a year. Even with papers in order, he or she could not vote, initiate a lawsuit or testify in court.

When Lincoln moved to Springfield in the spring of 1837, four of its residents owned slaves, despite the fact that Illinois was a free state. Several more held African Americans as indentured servants, a condition not far removed from slavery. And the majority of Springfield's citizens tacitly endorsed the state's restrictive black laws, which virtually stripped African Americans of legal rights.

SPRINGFIELD'S SLAVES AND INDENTURED SERVANTS

When Abraham Lincoln was twenty-two years old, he was hired to deliver a load of cargo down the Mississippi River to New Orleans. While there, he and his traveling companions came across a slave auction at which slaves were being "chained, maltreated—whipt & scourged," as his cousin recalled. Lincoln watched with horror as a young girl was pinched and prodded and examined like a horse by a coarse crowd of bidders. Revolted, Lincoln ushered his friends away, saying, "By God, boys, let's get away from this. If I ever get a chance to hit that thing [meaning slavery], I'll hit it hard." Many of Lincoln's friends and relatives believed that this incident was the start of Lincoln's lifelong aversion to slavery.

As it turned out, Lincoln was unable to get away from slavery, even when he returned to the ostensibly free state of Illinois. African Americans in Springfield were either slaves, servants or freed people whose rights were severely curtailed. However much Lincoln hated slavery, he was face to face with it (and its stepchild, indentured servitude) in his own hometown. Slaves and servants were present in the houses where he boarded, the houses he visited and the houses of his business associates. There were four slave owners in Springfield in 1840, and Lincoln knew three of them personally.

One of them was none other than William L. May, former congressman, current lawyer, future mayor of Springfield, Henry B. Truett's father-in-law—the same man who had once snuck into a friend's house in the middle of the night for illicit intercourse with his wife. May owned a female slave in her teens or early twenties named Bernice.

Another slaveholder Lincoln knew was storekeeper James Bell. When Lincoln came to town in 1837, Bell was employed by A.Y. Ellis and Company. He soon formed a dry goods partnership with Lincoln's best friend, Joshua Speed, with whom Lincoln lived until early 1841. Lincoln would represent James Bell, who owned a teenaged female slave, in more than two dozen debt collection cases throughout his career.

The third Springfield slaveholder in Lincoln's acquaintance was his future brother-in-law, Ninian Edwards. Lincoln had known Edwards since 1836, when they had served together in the Illinois General Assembly as part of the "long nine" delegation—so called because each of the representatives topped six feet tall. When he first moved to Springfield, Lincoln was a frequent guest in Edwards's home on Aristocracy Hill, the town's social center. It was there that he met Edwards's wife's sister, Mary Todd, who was visiting from Lexington, Kentucky. Lincoln spent many hours on the sofa in the parlor, listening spellbound as Mary enchanted him with her lively conversation and quick wit, perhaps having left his horse in the care of Edwards's teenaged male slave.

Ninian Edwards also had an African American indentured servant named Hepsey living in his house. She had been bound to him in 1835 at age eleven to "learn the art and mystery of domestic housewifery" until she reached the age of eighteen, agreeing to "serve his lawful secrets and commands" and to avoid "taverns alehouses tipling shops or houses of ill fame." In return, Edwards agreed to give her "good wholesome and sufficient meat drink washing lodging and apparel" and teach her to read and write (though not to do arithmetic—this was stricken from the contract). At the end of her term of service, Hepsey would have a new Bible and two new suits of clothes to show for seven years of labor. Hepsey might well have been in the Edwards house on November 4, 1842, when Lincoln and Mary Todd were married in the parlor.

Ninian Edwards was only one of several of Lincoln's friends and acquaintances who had indentured servants. John Todd, Mary Todd's uncle, had an indentured servant girl named Elizabeth. Henry B. Truett, the man whom Lincoln defended for the murder of Jacob Early in 1838, had a boy named James Shelby bound to service. Charles Dresser, the minister who married the Lincolns, had an indentured servant girl named Rhoda Jane. Virgil Hickox, whose milldam would be torn down in the hunt for Archibald Fisher's body and whom Lincoln represented in several legal cases, had James Shelby's brother John bound to him.

All of these indentured servants had agreed to a contract similar to Hepseys: they agreed to work until age eighteen (twenty-one for males), forgoing marriage and any trips to bars or whorehouses, in exchange for being taught the art of domestic labor, two suits of clothes and a Bible. In theory, their masters would treat them well, feed and clothe them, care for them in their illnesses and teach them to read and write. In reality, however, indentured servitude could be a miserable condition.

William May's servant Bernice, for example, was treated little better than chattel in 1841, when May gave her and her child to a woman named Felicia Kane to satisfy a debt. Henry Truett's servant James thought so little of Truett as a master that he ran away from service in 1840.

Perhaps James had received treatment similar to that dispensed by Dorothea Grant, a widow with two children who in 1843 was cited by her church for "UnChristian conduct, by treating a colored girl bound to her, with undue severity." It seems that Mrs. Grant, who admitted being in the habit of "correcting the girl when she thought her conduct required it," had whipped her with a cowhide a little too hard, leaving bruises on the poor girl's body. Mrs. Grant was puzzled; she didn't think she had whipped her "any more severely than she had done at other times." The only explanation that she could think of was that the cowhide she had used to whip her servant was "a different instrument" than the one she usually used, "the severe affect of which she was unconscious." At any rate, she acknowledged that "the whipping was too severe and not accompanied with that mercy which the Christian should always exercise" and said she was "sincerely sorry." This explanation was good enough for the church committee, which decided that, cowhide whipping notwithstanding, rumors that Mrs. Grant ill-treated her servant were "entirely unfounded."

It should be mentioned that Abraham Lincoln employed African American domestic servants within his own home. Unlike his friends and neighbors, however, Lincoln did not own them as slaves nor keep them as indentured servants. To the contrary, Lincoln's employees were paid wages in cash, they were free to come and go as they chose and there is every indication that he treated them with kindness and respect.

THE FUGITIVE SLAVE CASE

In 1839, a slave named Jim ran away from his master in Kentucky and headed north. In an effort to catch him, the master placed the following ad in Springfield's *Illinois State Register*:

> *Fifty Dollars Reward*
> *Ran away from the subscriber, living in Union county, Kentucky, on Saturday, the 22d day of June, a negro man, who calls himself Jim, about 31 years old, very black, 5 feet 11 inches high; can read and write very well; lips very thick, had on when he left a blue jeans frock coat, blue jeans vest, black fur hat; other clothing not recollected. The above reward will be given if taken anywhere in the State, or $100 if taken in any other State, and secured so that I get him again.*
> *Walter Barron, Union county, Ky.*

Notices like this were not uncommon in Springfield before the Civil War, as fugitive slaves passed through Springfield on their way north.

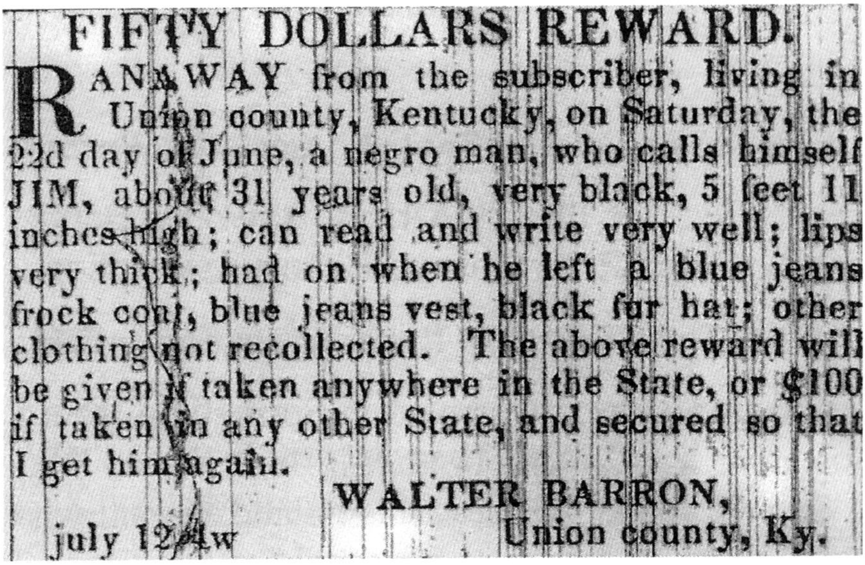

FIFTY DOLLARS REWARD.

RANAWAY from the subscriber, living in Union county, Kentucky, on Saturday, the 22d day of June, a negro man, who calls himself JIM, about 31 years old, very black, 5 feet 11 inches high; can read and write very well; lips very thick; had on when he left a blue jeans frock coat, blue jeans vest, black fur hat; other clothing not recollected. The above reward will be given if taken anywhere in the State, or $100 if taken in any other State, and secured so that I get him again.

WALTER BARRON,
Union county, Ky.

july 12 4w

Notices like this were not uncommon in Springfield before the Civil War, as fugitive slaves passed through Springfield on their way north. *Courtesy of* Illinois State Register, *August 10, 1839.*

Often the slaves passed safely through the city on their northward journey. Occasionally, the slaves were caught and sent back south, and the people who had harbored them were arrested.

Whatever the fate of these fugitives, their presence in Springfield stirred the passions of its residents. Situated in the center of Illinois, Springfield's population was composed of both northern- and southern-born citizens who mirrored pro- or antislavery biases found in the nation at large. Some, like Lincoln's law partner William H. Herndon, were zealous abolitionists agitating for an immediate end to slavery. Others, like Virginia-born lawyer Albert Bledsoe, were former slaveholders themselves who sympathized with the South and grew touchy over any perceived infringement on the right to own slaves. Still others, such as the Reverend Charles Dresser, president of the Springfield Colonization Society, sought the removal of African Americans to Africa. A good chunk of the population didn't particularly care for the institution of slavery but also didn't care for the idea of racial equality.

The issue of fugitive slaves took on national prominence when the Fugitive Slave Law was passed as part of the Compromise of 1850. This law required federal officials to actively help slave owners recover their fugitive slaves. Those officers who refused or failed to arrest a fugitive faced a fine of

$1,000, and those who successfully apprehended runaway slaves received a bonus. Anyone who provided food or shelter to a fugitive slave risked six months in jail and a fine of $1,000. Once caught, runaways were denied a trial by jury; instead they were hauled in front of a federal commissioner and, if their masters supplied sufficient evidence of ownership, returned from whence they came.

The new law sparked an uproar from abolitionists, who pointed out (rightly so) that many slaves would be kidnapped and sold into slavery so that unscrupulous federal marshals could collect bonuses, and resentment on the part of southerners, who often felt that those in the North weren't trying hard enough to uphold the law and return their runaways.

In July 1857, the town's citizens had their first opportunity to witness the Fugitive Slave Law in action when Frederick Clements was arrested on suspicion of being a runaway slave and brought before the U.S. commissioner in Springfield. Clements, forty-five years of age, was owned by Hiram McElroy of Union County, Kentucky. McElroy had frequently given him passes to visit his wife and children in southern Illinois; Clements had undertaken such a trip the past fall. In June, however, he had simply taken off, without warning and without permission. McElroy sent his son,

Northerners feared that the Fugitive Slave Law of 1850 would lead to runaway slaves being shot down like cattle and free blacks being kidnapped into slavery. *Courtesy of Library of Congress, Prints and Photographs Division.*

Hiram Jr., out to recover the missing slave. Knowing that Clements had family in Illinois, Hiram Jr. went looking for him there and finally tracked him to a farm outside of Atlanta, Illinois. Clements was immediately arrested and put into the custody of a U.S. marshal, who brought him to Springfield to await a hearing.

Springfield residents were extremely interested in seeing how the application of the Fugitive Slave Law would play out in Clements's case. Both pro- and antislavery camps hoped that the law would be upheld through a peaceable hearing, though for different reasons. The *Illinois State Register* hoped that the "insane raving of a few mad abolitionists or their fanatic clamor" would not prevent the hearing from ordering that the fugitive be returned to his rightful owner. The *Illinois State Journal*, on the other hand, hoped that the fugitive would find a fair hearing in Springfield and only be sent south if he was legally proved a slave, unlike in parts of southern Illinois where "they arrest without warrant or legal process, and shoot down negroes like cattle, if they resist." In this the *Journal* was correct; out of thirty-eight recorded fugitive slave apprehensions in Illinois after the passage of the law, twenty-seven were illegal abductions in which no hearing was held.

Given these grim facts, Frederick Clements was lucky to have a hearing at all and luckier still to be represented by an attorney, Lincoln's law partner William H. Herndon. A fierce opponent of slavery, with a slightly exaggerated sense of self-importance, Herndon had jumped at the chance to burnish his antislavery credentials by representing Clements. "I freely—quickly as well as freely, volunteered for the poor fellow," he proudly wrote to Theodore Parker, a prominent Boston minister and fellow abolitionist. Unable to resist expounding on his noble deed a little further, he wrote in a second letter to Parker: "In attending to that poor negro's case I felt I was doing my duty, and did not care for personal consequences, to myself."

He almost didn't get the chance to represent Clements. At the beginning of the trial, the opposing counsel coldly but quite correctly protested against the admission of an attorney for the fugitive slave. "Nobody," he argued, "has the right to contest the owner's claim to the negro. The court may admit counsel as advisory to itself, but not as attorneys for the alleged slave."

This was a slap in the face to Herndon. It was irritating enough that someone should try to bar his entry to the court. ("What have I done that I cannot appear in this court?" he had asked. "Are white men to be put down and divested of their rights as well as negroes?") Worse, however, was the fact that the opposing counsel who had delivered this injustice was none other than his own brother, Elliott Herndon, with whom he had in common

Left: Lincoln's law partner William H. Herndon, a zealous abolitionist, argued Springfield's first case under the Fugitive Slave Act. *Courtesy of Francis F. Browne's* The Every-day Life of Abraham Lincoln, *1886.*

Below: Theodore Parker, a prominent Boston abolitionist, learned of Springfield's fugitive slave case from William H. Herndon's self-congratulatory letters. *Courtesy of Library of Congress, Prints and Photographs Division.*

a last name and a profession but little else. "I came near having my own dear rights stricken down in court by my own brother," he complained to Parker. "I fought till I got my own rights. It was contended that I had no right to appear in court for the negro." Fortunately, Elliot's contention was no match for William's verbal prowess, at least in his own estimation. "I repelled this in language strong & manly, if I may say so," he concluded.

Notwithstanding Herndon's wounded pride, his brother was not out of line in pointing out that the fugitive slave required no legal representation. As unfair as it seems today, hearings conducted under the Fugitive Slave Laws were not like standard legal trials in which evidence was admitted from both sides and a verdict reached by a jury. On the contrary, during Fugitive Slave trials the slave was not allowed to testify, present evidence or provide a defense, and the commissioner was the lone decider. This being the case, Commissioner Stephen Corneau was being rather permissive by allowing Herndon to plead on Clements's behalf. For his part, Herndon was perfectly aware that he had almost no chance of securing Clements's freedom. He took the case not to win but to make noise and preach from the bully pulpit against the evils of the Fugitive Slave Law, probably to impress his abolitionist buddies in the East. He intimated as much when he sent newspaper clippings of the hearing to Parker and wrote, "Your, or any other good man's opinion has much to do with my acts."

Herndon, that bold crusader for slaves' rights, did what he could for Clements at the hearing, but there wasn't much he could do. Hiram McElroy Jr. testified that his father owned Frederick Clements and that Clements had run away without permission in June. One of McElroy's neighbors, who had accompanied Hiram Jr. to Illinois on his slave-catching trip, reiterated that Hiram McElroy owned Frederick Clements and identified the man in the courtroom as the slave in question. He also produced a power of attorney authorizing him to arrest and take possession of Clements to return him to Kentucky.

The case was open and shut, but Herndon did his best to keep it open. First he produced a series of passes McElroy's overseer had purportedly given Clements to travel to Illinois and argued that Clements had permission to be away. When Hiram Jr. countered that the overseer had no right to give out such passes, Herndon switched tracks and tried undermining the neighbor's power of attorney on a technicality, contending that it was invalid because it referred to Clements as a "fugitive of labor" and not explicitly as a "slave." When that didn't get him anywhere, he pulled out all the stops and claimed that the whole hearing was invalid because there was no proof that Kentucky was even a slave state. His brother (probably rolling his eyes and muttering "Oh, for God's sake" under his breath), protested that none of the points Herndon argued was even necessary to the commissioner's final decision.

After both sides made their closing arguments, the commissioner gave his verdict: Hiram Jr. had successfully proved that Clements was his father's legal property, and therefore Clements would be delivered up to his master in Kentucky. The audience in the packed courtroom took the verdict in stride. Many of them might have disagreed with the Fugitive Slave Law, but they could not argue with the fact that the rule of law had been upheld, and peaceably at that.

At least two people in Springfield were not pleased with the verdict. One of them, obviously, was poor Frederick Clements, who after briefly having tasted freedom was being taken back to Kentucky in chains. The other was William H. Herndon, would-be abolitionist crusader, who had done his best for the cause and still came up short. Not that it was his fault, Herndon decided. After all, the commissioner of the hearing stood to make ten dollars if the slave was returned to his master. "The poor negro was tried and sent south—could not prevent it," he wrote bitterly to Parker. And then, philosophically, "You cannot do any good when…the 10 dolls. are gingling in the ears of the hell-gopher Commissioner."

Chapter 5

ABRAHAM LINCOLN'S SCANDAL

Today, Abraham Lincoln is remembered as much for his magnanimity as for his remarkable presidency. But the man who wrote "with malice towards none, with charity for all" had some rough edges in his youth that were only smoothed out with age and experience. Lincoln was a talented storyteller, speaker and writer. Most of the time, he used these talents for the betterment of his political party and his country. Occasionally, though, as a young man, he used his sharp wit and sharper words to puncture the egos of his political opponents and personal rivals. Occasionally, this behavior got him in trouble. And one time, it could have cost him his life.

THE POISON PEN

Abraham Lincoln had been telling stories practically all his life. His childhood friends remembered how he would have the neighborhood laughing with the tales he told, his talent for mimicry, his awkward yet enthusiastic gestures and his unparalleled ability to deliver a punch line. This storytelling ability helped him to make friends when he arrived in New Salem as a penniless and friendless twenty-one-year-old boy. It also helped him to be successful in the courtroom when addressing juries and in politics as a stump speaker. Lincoln had a way of explaining even the most complicated issues in a way that everyone could understand the logic of his points, and he often peppered his speeches with jokes and stories that kept his crowds in stitches.

Occasionally, however, when rebutting a point someone else had made, he crossed the line from professional argument to personal ridicule. Once during a legal case, Lincoln mocked his opposing counsel before the jury by pointing out that his shirt was on backward. Lincoln remarked that this man might have been a very knowing lawyer, but he couldn't have been all that smart if he couldn't even manage to put his clothes on correctly. On the stump, his words could be even more biting. Several of Lincoln's friends recalled times when he had "skinned" his political adversaries, deriding them to the point of mortification or worse.

Probably no one received a more severe tongue-lashing from Lincoln than Jesse B. Thomas, a Democratic politician and former law partner of William L. May. During the heated presidential race of 1840, Thomas actively campaigned for Martin van Buren and the Democratic Party, while Lincoln campaigned for William Henry Harrison and the Whigs. At one point, after listening to Thomas deliver a speech on the steps of the Sangamon County Circuit Court, Lincoln stood up and lit into him mercilessly, mimicking him, mocking his voice and aping his gestures to the crowd's extreme amusement. Thomas was so humiliated that he began to cry, right there in front of everyone. To his credit, Lincoln afterward felt terrible for having upset Thomas so and apologized to him.

Lincoln's ridicule was not just confined to the courtroom or the political stump. In his younger years, he was also the frequent author of anonymous letters to the *Sangamo Journal* that skewered his political opponents, much to their irritation and chagrin. No sooner had Lincoln hit town in the spring of 1837 than he started up one such anonymous attack in the pages of the *Journal*. The object of his scorn was James Adams, an admittedly shady character who had fled New York on charges that he had forged a deed to six hundred acres of land. Now, in Springfield, Lincoln believed that Adams had forged another deed to a tract of land claimed by one of Lincoln's clients, a widow by the name of Mary Anderson. But what really got Lincoln's goat, more than allegedly defrauding a poor widow out of her inheritance, was the fact that Adams was running for the position of probate judge against Lincoln's good friend Anson G. Henry.

With the help of his fellow Whig lawyers, Lincoln wrote a series of letters under the name of "Sampson's Ghost" that tore into Adams, accusing him of forging the deed in question. He also called Adams a Tory. Adams quite perceptively surmised that Lincoln was the author

In his younger days, Abraham Lincoln's sharp tongue occasionally caused hurt feelings and bruised egos. *Courtesy of Library of Congress, Prints and Photographs Division.*

of the letters and retorted that the whole issue had been conjured up to harm his chances in the upcoming election. He also called Lincoln a deist. Lincoln, dropping the pseudonym, replied with a handbill and two public letters, dismantling Adams's rebuttals point by point and finishing by calling Adams, in essence, a whiner.

Ultimately, the political pissing contest touched off by Lincoln's "Sampson's Ghost" letters did nothing except make Lincoln look unprofessional. Adams defeated Anson Henry for probate judge and also held on to the land in question until his death in 1843. It would take one more foray into the murky waters of anonymous newspaper attacks and wanton character assassination before Lincoln learned his lesson and abandoned the practice for good. In 1842, Lincoln once again dipped his pen into the ink of gall and went after a Democratic adversary with an anonymous letter to the newspaper. This time, however, his adversary pushed back.

James Shields, the Democratic Illinois state auditor, was a hot-tempered, smooth-tongued Irishman with a soft spot for ladies and fancy ruffled shirts. When the State Bank of Illinois went under in the fall of 1842, Shields was put in the unenviable position of having to refuse its worthless bank notes as payment for taxes, sparking outcry among the general population who had scant access to gold and silver. This was all the opening Lincoln needed to go after Shields and the Democratic Party (but especially Shields). A political rival who would undoubtedly challenge Lincoln's Whig party for important office in the future, Shields's vanity apparently also rubbed Lincoln the wrong way on a personal level. Lincoln took the opportunity to vent his spleen publicly.

Once again, Lincoln took to the pages of the *Sangamo Journal*, this time lampooning his foe under the guise of "Rebecca," a plain yet clever farm wife who lived out in the country in the fictional "Lost Townships." To be fair, he hadn't started this attack. Someone else had created the Rebecca character and submitted letters to the *Sangamo Journal* under her name throughout 1838. The author of those earlier letters had turned his wit against the Democratic Party with a Rebecca letter on August 10. But where this author only alluded to Shields indirectly in the second to last paragraph of his lengthy and somewhat dull letter, Lincoln's lively "Rebecca" letter of September 2 singled Shields out by name.

The tone of Lincoln's letter was in general a little more risqué than the previous author's dry, rambling prose. He opened with Rebecca setting out to visit neighbors who had just had a new baby. Rebecca came across the father, Jeff, sitting outside reading a newspaper. When Rebecca inquired how he was, Jeff replied that he was mad as the devil. Lincoln's Rebecca gave the following suggestive reply: "'What about,' says I, 'aint its hair the right color? None of that nonsense, Jeff—there aint an honester woman in the Lost Township than—'"

Illinois state auditor James Shields challenged Lincoln to a duel in 1842. *Courtesy of Library of Congress, Prints and Photographs Division.*

It turns out that Jeff was angry that the state bank was refusing bank notes and demanding gold or silver for payment of taxes. Lincoln's two characters discussed the situation in their rough dialects. When they spotted a notice in the paper written by Shields with which they disagreed, Lincoln's Jeff voiced his frustration in the following diatribe: "Shields is a fool as well as a liar. With him truth is out of the question, and as for getting a good bright passable lie out of him, you might as well try to strike fire from a cake of tallow."

Clearly, Lincoln had crossed the line and made his political argument a personal attack by calling Shields a fool and a liar. But he wasn't done yet. Taking a stab at Shields's reputation as a flirt, Lincoln penned the following fictional account of Jeff's observation of Shields at a fair:

> *All the galls about town was there, and all the handsome widows, and married women, finickin about, trying to look like galls, tied as tight in the middle, and puffed out at both ends like bundles of fodder that hadn't been stacked yet, but wanted stackin pretty bad. And then they had tables all round the house kivered over with baby caps, and pin-cushions, and ten thousand such little nicknacks, tryin to sell 'em to the fellows that were bowin and scrapin, and kungeerin about 'em…I looked in at the window, and there was this same*

> *fellow Shields floatin about on the air, without heft or earthly substance, just like a lock of cat-fur where cats had been fightin.*
>
> *He was paying his money to this one and that one, and tother one, and sufferin great loss because it wasn't silver instead of State paper; and the sweet distress he seemed to be in,—his very features, in the exstatic agony of his soul, spoke audibly and distinctly—"Dear girls,* it is distressing, *but I cannot marry you all. Too well I know how much you suffer; but do,* do *remember, it is not my fault that I am* so *handsome and* so *interesting."*
>
> *As this last was expressed by a most exquisite contortion of his face, he seized hold of one of their hands and squeezed, and held on to it about a quarter of an hour.*

Although Lincoln had made some salient points about the impracticality of forbidding state bank notes as payment for taxes, he had also kicked Shields right where it hurt, in his pride. Shields fancied himself both a man of good character (which by all accounts he was) and a ladies' man, and Lincoln's letter in the newspaper had made him seem ridiculous on both accounts. Worse still, other people were jumping on the bandwagon. Another letter by Rebecca criticizing Shields appeared in the *Sangamo Journal* on September 9, followed by a fourth, by far the most offensive, on September 16.

James Shields was humiliated. All of Springfield was laughing at him. Moreover, he was enraged. He wanted retribution for his mistreatment. In antebellum America, that meant only one thing. Shields was going to find out just who the author of the letters was. And when he did, that person would have two choices: take back everything he had said against Shields or fight a duel.

THE DUEL

Two weeks after he had anonymously called Shields a fool and a liar in the *Sangamo Journal*, Abraham Lincoln was attending court in Tremont, Illinois. On the morning of Saturday, September 16, Lincoln was preparing to head into the courtroom to represent George R. Justice and George M. Justice in a debt recovery case when he was surprised by the appearance of two friends just arrived from Springfield. The news they brought was serious: James Shields was hot on their heels and spoiling for a fight with Lincoln.

Shields, it seemed, had gone to the editor of the *Sangamo Journal* and demanded the name of the person responsible for writing the letters that had made him a laughingstock in town. Obligingly, the editor gave up Lincoln's name. Shields, angry and humiliated and unwilling to wait several weeks for Lincoln's return from the legal circuit, was on his way to Tremont to challenge Lincoln to a duel. Elias Merryman and William Butler had ridden through the night to reach Lincoln first, knowing very well that Lincoln was totally ignorant of the practice of dueling. They hoped to prevent Lincoln from making a blunder that could cost him his honor or his life.

They needn't have worried. Lincoln had no desire to get killed, and he'd been preparing himself for the possibility that Shields would issue a challenge to duel since the letter had been published. Coached by his friend Albert Bledsoe, Lincoln had been training with cavalry sabers, figuring that he stood a better chance of coming out of a duel alive if no pistols were involved. He was reasonably certain that, if a duel occurred, he could use his long arms and superior physical strength to disarm his opponent before either of them came to harm.

Merryman asked Lincoln what he was planning to do with the mess he now had on his hands. Lincoln replied that he was wholly opposed to dueling and would do everything in his power to avoid such a confrontation, as long as he could do so without damaging his own honor. If he had to make a choice between suffering personal degradation or fighting, however, he would choose fighting. Elias Merryman was probably the wrong person to admit this to, as he had a definite reckless streak (this is the same Elias Merryman who had been checking James Brown's windowsill for love letters from his wife Maria two years earlier). William Butler was no better and possibly worse; he was itching to see a fight, the sooner the better. No one will ever know for sure, but it is possible that these two hotheads had a hand in convincing Lincoln that there was no honorable way to duck this fight.

Not long after Merryman and Butler reached Lincoln, Shields and his friend John D. Whiteside arrived in Tremont. Without delay, Whiteside approached Lincoln bearing a note from the aggrieved state auditor. This was all quite proper, according to the gentlemen's code of dueling, which stipulated that the offended party should first attempt to negotiate a peaceful resolution through the exchange of letters. Shields's note to Lincoln, however, was heavy on threat and light on attempts at reconciliation. In it, he demanded "a full positive and absolute retraction of all offensive allusions used by you in these communications, in relation to my private character and standing as a man, as an apology for the insults conveyed in them." He added, ominously, "This may prevent consequences which no one will regret more than myself." It was now patently clear that Lincoln's unprovoked use of the poison pen had landed him in a heap of trouble.

Mortal danger notwithstanding, with his two firebrand friends egging him on, Lincoln refused to capitulate. Instead, he sent a note back to Shields at sunset that evening expressing his irritation that Shields had demanded an unqualified retraction of the offensive letters and floated the specter of a duel "without stopping to enquire whether I really am the author, or to point out what is offensive in them." He concluded, haughtily, that Shields's letter contained "so much assumption of facts, and so much of menace as to consequences, that I cannot submit to answer that note any farther than I have."

The ball was now back in Shields's court. In about an hour's time, Whiteside returned with a second note from Shields to Lincoln, this one milder in tone, asking if Lincoln was the author of the Rebecca letters and repeating his request for a retraction of the offensive content. It didn't reach Lincoln. William Butler intercepted Whiteside before he could deliver it and declared that Lincoln had no interest in reading anything Shields wrote unless it was a retraction of his first note or a challenge to duel. If Lincoln truly was interested in avoiding a duel, he probably should have chosen someone else to do his negotiating for him. As it was, Whiteside had no choice but to go back to Shields with the news that his second note had been rebuffed and try to persuade him to retract his first note.

This Shields refused to do. He, after all, was the injured party—Lincoln had used the newspaper to humiliate him publicly! Who did Lincoln think he was, now pretending to be offended by Shields's private note? Lincoln, for his part, also refused to budge, even after Butler finally showed him the second note. He had decided, either on his own or with the input of his friends, that Shields's first note was so egregious that Shields must either retract it or meet him on the field of honor.

Shields chose the latter. By now it was the only recourse; both he and Lincoln had their heels dug in. Shields named Whiteside as his second, the person who would keep calm and negotiate all the particulars of the conflict on his behalf. Lincoln, in turn, named Merryman as his own second, probably as the lesser of two evils; between Merryman and Butler, Merryman had the slightly cooler head. The two seconds conferred with each other, both agreeing that it would be nice if Shields would retract his first note so the whole affair could be settled amicably. Whiteside, however, was not optimistic. He had been trying to encourage Shields to do just that for two days now, without luck. In fact, Whiteside went on to say that it would be best if Shields never found out that Whiteside had been trying to negotiate peace at all. "He would challenge me next, and as soon cut my throat as not," he confided. Merryman was impressed; Shields sounded like a badass. It wouldn't do for Lincoln to come off like a sissy in this situation, so Merryman promised not to say anything to either party, letting the implication hang in the air that Lincoln, too, was dangerous and not to be trifled with.

Lincoln, Merryman, Butler and Whiteside arrived back in Springfield on Monday evening only to learn that the news of the duel had beaten them home, while Shields, whose horse was lame, was still plodding along the road from Tremont. Now the whole town was buzzing with talk of an affair of honor between the fiery state auditor and the up-and-coming young lawyer. Worse, the local authorities were making ominous noises about arresting Lincoln and Shields, as dueling was illegal in Illinois. Lincoln decided to get the heck out of dodge rather than risk arrest, as issuing or accepting a challenge to duel was punishable by stiff fines, and an actual duel (provided one survived) could result in five years in prison. On Tuesday morning, he packed a bag and lit out for Jacksonville, where he would borrow a pair of broadswords from the encamped state militia's cavalry and wait for his friends to join him.

Before leaving, he handed Merryman a memorandum of instructions for the duel. His first paragraph expressed his willingness to back down, if Shields would retract his note, and explained that his newspaper letters were written for political effect and not from personal spite. Knowing full well that Shields would not retract his note, Lincoln went on to spell out his terms.

As the challenged party, Lincoln had the privilege of choosing the weapons, position, time and place of the conflict. The weapons were a no-brainer. Lincoln later explained to a friend why he had chosen broadswords: "To tell you the truth, Linder, I did not want to kill Shields, and felt sure that I could disarm him, having had about a month to learn the broadsword exercise; and furthermore, I didn't want the damned fellow to kill me, which I rather think he would have done if we had selected pistols." To bolster his chances with the broadswords, Lincoln declared that a plank would be placed between the two combatants and that neither could come within approximately six feet of it. At this distance, Shields would be at a distinct disadvantage to Lincoln's long arms.

Lincoln chose United States cavalry broadswords as his dueling weapon, hoping to keep James Shields at bay with his long arms. *Courtesy of Library of Congress, Prints and Photographs Division.*

Lincoln decided that Thursday, September 22, at 5:00 p.m. would be a good time to engage in mortal combat. This would give all parties time to reach the island on the Missouri side of the Mississippi River that he had selected as the location of the duel. It was a popular place to fight; the island, just across the river from Alton, Illinois, had been dubbed "Bloody Island" by other Illinoisans who had gone there to duel on the safe side of the law.

After Lincoln left, Merryman prevailed on Whiteside one more time to talk Shields into retracting his note but got nowhere. Whiteside flatly told him that Shields would sooner "butt his brains out against a brick wall as to withdraw that paper." With no further recourse, all parties struck out for Bloody Island. Shields's group, which included himself, Whiteside, John Ewing and Thomas Hope, got there shortly before eleven o'clock on Thursday morning. Lincoln's group, composed of himself, Merryman, Butler and Albert Bledsoe, arrived not long after.

The air was thick with tension. Most duels of that time were peacefully resolved long before the parties actually faced off against each other; the fact that both had arrived on Bloody Island with weapons in hand was ominous. Lincoln, coat and vest removed, cleared the underbrush with an axe and took a few practice swipes at the bushes with his sword. Shields sat nearby and watched his unusually strong opponent swing his disproportionately long arms, probably wondering how Whiteside could be so incompetent as to agree to weapons that left him at such a disadvantage.

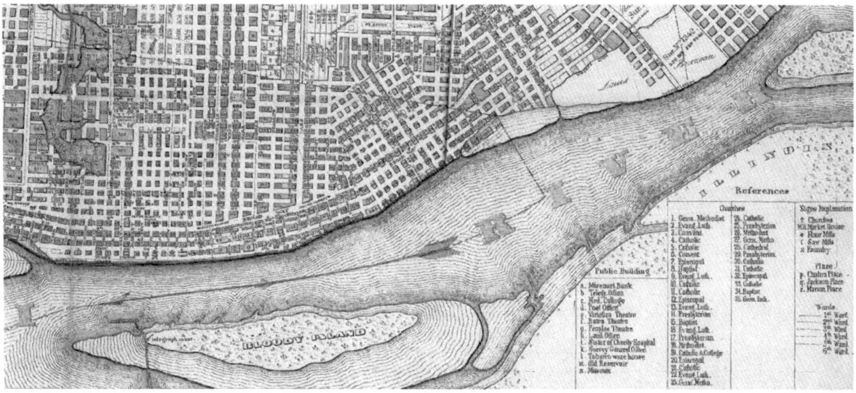

Because dueling was illegal in Illinois, Lincoln and Shields went to Bloody Island, Missouri, for their duel. *Courtesy of* Map of the City of St. Louis and Vicinity, *Drawn and Engraved by J.H. Fisher, 1853.*

At last, the parties were ready to begin. Both took up their swords and took a deep breath.

But before they could take a swing, John J. Hardin and Revel W. English swept onto the scene. Hardin was a young, handsome and popular Whig, and English was a levelheaded Democrat. Together, they urged all parties to try one more time to reach a peaceful accord. Not particularly wanting to see their friend cut to ribbons, Whiteside and company, on Shields's behalf but without his knowledge, retracted the note that he had written. Obligingly, Merryman declared that Lincoln's "Rebecca" letter had been written solely for political effect and that Lincoln had not intended any malice or offense. And just like that, the duel was over.

William Butler couldn't believe it. He had been sitting on a log some thirty feet away, expecting to see a bloody fight, when all of a sudden the swords were taken out of Lincoln's and Shields's hands and everyone was preparing to depart. In fact, the two would-be combatants now seemed to be on amiable terms. They had even conspired to dress a log in a red shirt, leading the anxious people on the Alton shore to assume that one of them was returning cut to bloody pieces. Butler was sorely disappointed.

Happily for Butler, two weeks later, Shields (also apparently still in a fighting mood) challenged *him* to a duel. This time there would be no messing around with broadswords in Missouri, either. Butler would be ready to go with rifles at one hundred yards in Bob Allen's meadow outside

Springfield the next day at dawn. Only the intervention of Whiteside, once again acting as Shields's second, stopped this duel from happening. Whiteside may not have been savvy enough to insist on a fair selection of weapons in the Lincoln duel, but at least he knew enough to prevent a duel from taking place in a state where the crime was punishable by jail.

The appetite for dueling in Springfield was not quite sated, however. The day after the Shields-Butler duel fizzled, Whiteside challenged Merryman to a duel, this one stemming from salvos they had exchanged in the *Sangamo Journal* while explaining the circumstances of the Lincoln-Shields duel. Merryman tapped Lincoln as his second, while Whiteside chose Shields, in an ironic inversion of the original duel. This last duel failed to come off, as well, when the combatants couldn't agree on a time and place to meet.

After the dust had settled and tempers had cooled, Lincoln came to view his abortive duel with embarrassment and regret and tried to forget that it had ever happened. More than twenty years later, a visitor to the White House asked President Lincoln if it was true that he had once accepted a challenge to duel. Lincoln flushed angrily and snapped, "I do not deny it, but if you desire my friendship you will never mention the circumstance again!"

Abraham Lincoln had finally learned the consequences of personally ridiculing others in public speeches and writings. Henceforward, he tempered his words and generally turned his mockery to himself for humorous effect.

Chapter 6

MURDER MOST FOUL

On the whole, Lincoln's Springfield was a relatively peaceful town. Neighbors drove one another crazy and stepped on one another's toes, to be sure, but they usually employed legal action and not violence to settle their disputes. Occasionally, ragged nerves or an overindulgence of whiskey led to the odd fistfight, but most of the time both parties walked away with only bumps and bruises. Most of the time.

Every so often, however, someone would introduce a knife into a fistfight, or someone's frayed temper would finally snap and he would reach for his gun. Or a body would turn up with a hole in its head or a handkerchief tied over its face. The people of Springfield were only human, after all, and every so often humans get mad and kill one another.

When a murder occurred, it was big news in town—it "caused great excitement," in the parlance of the day. People talked over backyard fences and formed opinions long before the trial officially declared innocence or guilt. Occasionally, a murder made the townspeople mad enough to kill (ironically), and only incarceration kept the accused safe from the threat of vigilante justice. Defending attorneys in murder cases notoriously moved for changes of venue, hoping to move the trial someplace where emotions didn't run quite as high.

Like the murders themselves, murder trials caused great excitement in Springfield. Often the courtrooms were packed with spectators eager to hear the lurid details of the testimony and to learn the fate of the accused. By law, a guilty verdict would result in a sentence to hang, which only made the proceedings that much more compelling. Those who didn't attend court in person followed the trial in the newspapers, where high-profile cases commanded several columns' worth of newsprint each day.

As an attorney, Lincoln was directly involved with twenty-five murder cases over the course of his career. Indirectly, he almost certainly learned the details of every murder in Springfield from the attorneys who tried the cases, from reading the newspapers or from sitting in the courtroom during the trials. What follows are four of the most wicked murders in Springfield's history.

THE TRAILOR MYSTERY: THE MURDER THAT WASN'T

On June 6, 1841, a small notice appeared in Springfield's *Sangamo Journal*:

> *TO THE PUBLIC.*
> *A Man by the name of Fisher, arrived in this city on Monday last from Warren County, with the undersigned, and has not been seen or heard of since about 6 o'clock that day. He is at times deranged, caused by an injury on the head. He is about 35 or 40 years of age, 5 foot 10 inches high, sandy whiskers, black hair—had on a blue broad-cloth coat, brown jeans pantaloons, and a white fur hat about half worn. He is a carpenter by trade. Any person knowing any thing of the above man, will much oblige his friends by leaving word at this office, or at the subscriber's residence, in Clary's Grove.*
> *HENRY TRAILER*

Little did Springfield's citizens realize the hornet's nest of intrigue and false accusation that would be stirred up by the disappearance of poor, deranged Archibald Fisher. Within two weeks, however, the community was in an uproar, convinced that Fisher was dead and that Henry Trailor, along with his brothers William and Archibald, had killed him. Long on righteous indignation but short on facts, an angry mob turned the countryside upside down looking for the body. It was all to no avail, for there was no body to find; as it turned out, Archibald Fisher was not dead at all.

Abraham Lincoln observed his townsmen's overblown reaction with unconcealed amusement. On June 19, he sat down to write his best friend the news from Springfield, telling him, "We have had the highest state of excitement here for a week past that our community has ever witnessed" and filling him in on the details of how his fellow townsmen had swept away "like a herd of buffaloes, and cut down Hickoxes mill dam nolens volens, to draw the water out of the pond; and then went up and down, and down and up the creek, fishing and raking, and ducking and diving for two days" looking for the body of the "supposed murderee."

Lincoln himself had been drawn into the fracas when he and his partner, Stephen T. Logan, were hired as defense attorneys by the Trailor brothers, who had been arrested and arraigned before the Sangamon County justice of the peace. As such, he had a front-row seat to watch the reactions of his overly excited townsmen when the surprise announcement came that Fisher was alive all the while. As Lincoln recalled:

> *Some looked quizical, some melancholly, and some furiously angry. Porter, who had been very active, swore he always knew the man was not dead, and that he had not stirred an inch to hunt for him; Langford, who had taken the lead in cuting down Hickoxes mill dam, and wanted to hang Hickox for objecting, looked most awfully wo-begone;...and Hart, the little drayman that hauled Molly home once, said it was too damned bad, to have so much trouble, and no hanging after all.*

He was so tickled by the incident that five years later he wrote up an account of the hullaballoo and had it published in the newspaper. What follows is the story in Lincoln's own words, as it appeared in the *Quincy Whig* on April 15, 1846:

> *Remarkable Case of Arrest for Murder*
>
> *In the year 1841, there resided, at different points in the State of Illinois, three brothers by the name of Trailor. Their Christian names were William, Henry and Archibald. Archibald resided at Springfield, then as now the seat of Government of the State. He was a sober, retiring, and industrious man, of about thirty years of age; a carpenter by trade, and a bachelor, boarding with his partner in business—a Mr. Myers. Henry, a year or two older, was a man of like retiring and industrious habits; had a family, and resided with it on a farm, at Clary's Grove, about twenty miles distant from Springfield in a northwesterly direction.—William, still older, and with similar habits, resided on a farm in Warren county, distant from Springfield*

something more than a hundred miles in the same North-westerly direction. He was a widower, with several children.

In the neighborhood of William's residence, there was, and had been for several years, a man by the name of Fisher, who was somewhat above the age of fifty; had no family, and no settled home; but who boarded and lodged a while here and a while there, with persons for whom he did little jobs of work. His habits were remarkably economical, so that an impression got about that he had accumulated a considerable amount of money.

In the latter part of May, in the year mentioned, William formed the purpose of visiting his brothers at Clary's Grove and Springfield; and Fisher, at the time having his temporary residence at his house, resolved to accompany him. They set out together in a buggy with a single horse. On Sunday evening they reached Henry's residence, and staid over night. On Monday morning, being the first Monday of June, they started on to Springfield, Henry accompanying them on horseback. They reached town about noon, met Archibald, went with him to his boarding house, and there took up their lodgings for the time they should remain.

After dinner, the three Trailers and Fisher left the boarding house in company, for the avowed purpose of spending the evening together in looking about the town. At supper, the Trailers had all returned, but Fisher was missing, and some inquiry was made about him. After supper, the Trailers went out professedly in search of him. One by one they returned, the last coming in after late tea time, and each stating that he had been unable to discover anything of Fisher.

The next day, both before and after breakfast, they went professedly in search again, and returned at noon, still unsuccessful. Dinner again being had, William and Henry expressed a determination to give up the search, and start for their homes. This was remonstrated against by some of the boarders about the house, on the ground that Fisher was somewhere in the vicinity, and would be left without any conveyance, as he and William had come in the same buggy. The remonstrance was disregarded, and they departed for their homes respectively.

Up to this time, the knowledge of Fisher's mysterious disappearance had spread very little beyond the few boarders at Myers', and excited no considerable interest. After the lapse of three or four days, Henry returned to Springfield, for the ostensible purpose of makings further search for Fisher. Procuring some of the boarders, he, together with them and Archibald, spent another day in ineffectual search, when it was again abandoned, and he returned home.

No general interest was yet excited.

On the Friday, week after Fisher's disappearance, the Postmaster at Springfield received a letter from the Postmaster nearest William's residence, in Warren county, stating that William had returned home without Fisher, and was saying, rather boastfully, that Fisher was dead, and had willed him his money, and that he had got about fifteen hundred dollars by it. The letter further stated that William's story and conduct seemed strange, and desired the Postmaster at Springfield to ascertain and write what was the truth in the matter.

The Postmaster at Springfield made the letter public, and at once, excitement became universal and intense. Springfield, at that time, had a population of about 3,500, with a city organization. The Attorney General of the State resided there. A purpose was forthwith formed to ferret out the mystery, in putting which into execution, the Mayor of the city and the Attorney General took the lead. To make search for, and, if possible, find the body of the man supposed to be murdered, was resolved on as the first step.

In pursuance of this, men were formed into large parties, and marched abreast, in all directions, so as to let no inch of ground in the vicinity remain unsearched. Examinations were made of cellars, wells, and pits of all descriptions, where it was thought possible the body might be concealed. All the fresh, or tolerably fresh graves in the graveyard, were pried into, and dead horses and dead dogs were disintered, where, in some instances, they had been buried by their partial masters.

This search, as has appeared, commenced on Friday. It continued until Saturday afternoon without success, when it was determined to despatch officers to arrest William and Henry, at their residences, respectively. The officers started on Sunday morning, meanwhile, the search for the body was continued, and rumors got afloat of the Trailors having passed, at different times and places, several gold pieces, which were readily supposed to have belonged to Fisher.

On Monday, the officers sent for Henry, having arrested him, arrived with him. The Mayor and Attorney Gen'l took charge of him, and set their wits to work to elicit a discovery from him. He denied, and denied, and persisted in denying. They still plied him in every conceivable way, till Wednesday, when, protesting his own innocence, he stated that his brothers, William and Archibald, had murdered Fisher; that they had killed him, without his (Henry's) knowledge at the time, and made a temporary concealment of his body; that, immediately preceding his and William's departure from

Springfield for home, on Tuesday, the day after Fisher's disappearance, William and Archibald communicated the fact to him, and engaged his assistance in making a permanent concealment of the body; that, at the time he and William left professedly for home, they did not take the road directly, but, meandering their way through the streets, entered the woods at the North West of the city, two or three hundred yards to the right of where the road they should have travelled, entered them; that, penetrating the woods some few hundred yards, they halted and Archibald came a somewhat different route, on foot, and joined them; that William and Archibald then stationed him (Henry) on an old and disused road that ran near by, as a sentinel, to give warning of the approach of any intruder; that William and Archibald then removed the buggy to the edge of a dense brush thicket, about forty yards distant from his (Henry's) position, where, leaving the buggy, they entered the thicket, and in a few minutes returned with the body, and placed it in the buggy; that from his station he could and did distinctly see that the object placed in the buggy was a dead man, of the general appearance and size of Fisher; that William and Archibald then moved off with the buggy in the direction of Hickox's mill pond, and after an absence of half an hour, returned, saying they had put him in a safe place; that Archibald then left for town, and he and William found their way to the road, and made for their homes.

At this disclosure, all lingering credulity was broken down, and excitement rose to an almost inconceivable height. Up to this time the well-known character of Archibald had repelled and put down all suspicions as to him. Till then, those who were ready to swear that a murder had been committed, were almost as confident that Archibald had had no part in it. But now, he was seized and thrown into jail; and indeed, his personal security rendered it by no means objectionable to him.

And now came the search for the brush thicket, and the search of the mill pond. The thicket was found, and the buggy tracks at the point indicated. At a point within the thicket, the signs of a struggle were discovered, and a trail from thence to the buggy track was traced. In attempting to follow the track of the buggy from the thicket, it was found to proceed in the direction of the mill pond, but could not be traced all the way. At the pond, however, it was found that a buggy had been backed down to, and partially into the water's edge.

Search was now to be made in the pond; and it was made in every imaginable way. Hundreds and hundreds were engaged in raking, fishing, and draining. After much fruitless effort in this way, on Thursday morning the mill dam was cut down, and the water of the pond partially drawn off, and the same processes of search again gone through with.

About noon of this day, the officer sent for William, returned having him in custody; and a man calling himself Dr. Gilmore, came in company with them. It seems that the officer arrested William at his own house, early in the day on Tuesday, and started to Springfield with him; that after dark awhile, they reached Lewiston, in Fulton county, where they stopped for the night; that late in the night this Dr. Gilmore arrived, stating that Fisher was alive at his house, and that he had followed on to give the information, so that William might be released without further trouble; that the officer, distrusting Dr. Gilmore, refused to release William, but brought him on to Springfield, and the Dr. accompanied them.

On reaching Springfield, the Dr. re-asserted that Fisher was alive, and at his house. At this, the multitude for a time, were utterly confounded. Gilmore's story was communicated to Henry Trailor, who without faltering, reaffirmed his own story about Fisher's murder. Henry's adherence to his own story was communicated to the crowd, and at once the idea started, and became nearly, if not quite universal, that Gilmore was a confederate of the Trailors, and had invented the tale he was telling, to secure their release and escape.

Excitement was again at its zenith.

About three o'clock the same evening, Myers, Archibald's partner, started with a two-horse carriage, for the purpose of ascertaining whether Fisher was alive, as stated by Gilmore, and if so, of bringing him back to Springfield with him.

On Friday a legal examination was gone into before two Justices, on the charge of murder against William and Archibald. Henry was introduced as a witness by the prosecution, and on oath re-affirmed his statements, as heretofore detailed, and at the end of which he bore a thorough and rigid cross-examination without faltering or exposure. The prosecution also proved, by a respectable lady, that on the Monday evening of Fisher's disappearance, she saw Archibald, whom she well knew, and another man whom she did not then know, but whom she believed at the time of testifying to be William, (then present), and still another, answering the description of Fisher, all enter the timber at the North West of town, (the point indicated by Henry), and after one or two hours, saw William and Archibald return without Fisher.

Several other witnesses testified, that on Tuesday, at the time William and Henry professedly gave up the search for Fishers body, and started for home, they did not take the road directly, but did go into the woods, as stated by Henry. By others, also, it was proved, that since Fisher's disappearance, William and Archibald had passed rather an unusual number of gold pieces. The statements heretofore made about the thicket, the signs of a struggle, the buggy tracks, &c., were fully proven by numerous witnesses.

At this the prosecution rested.

Dr. Gilmore was then introduced by the defendants. He stated that he resided in Warren county, about seven miles distant from William's residence; that on the morning of William's arrest, he was out from home, and heard of the arrest, and of its being on a charge of the murder of Fisher; that on returning to his own house, he found Fisher there; that Fisher was in very feeble health, and could give no rational account as to where he had been during his absence; that he (Gilmore) then started in pursuit of the officer, as before stated; and that he should have taken Fisher with him, only that the state of his health did not permit. Gilmore also stated that he had known Fisher for several years, and that he had understood he was subject to temporary derangement of mind, owing to an injury about his head received in early life.

There was about Dr. Gilmore so much of the air and manner of truth, that his statement prevailed in the minds of the audience and of the court, and the Trailors were discharged, although they attempted no explanation of the circumstances proven by the other witnesses.

On the next Monday, Myers arrived in Springfield, bringing him the now famed Fisher, in full life and proper person.

Thus ended this strange affair and while it is readily conceived that a writer of novels could bring a story to a more perfect climax, it may well be doubted whether a stranger affair ever really occurred. Much of the matter remains in mystery to this day. The going into the woods with Fisher, and returning without him, by the Trailers; their going into the woods at the same place the next day, after they professed to have given up the search; the signs of a struggle in the thicket, the buggy tracks at the edge of it; and the location of the thicket, and the signs about it, corresponding precisely with Henry's story, are circumstances that have never been explained. William and Archibald have both died since—William in less than a year, and Archibald in about two years after the supposed murder. Henry is still living, but never speaks of the subject.

It is not the object of the writer of this to enter into the many curious speculations that might be indulged upon the facts of this narrative; yet he can scarcely forbear a remark upon what would, almost certainly, have been the fate of William and Archibald, had Fisher not been found alive. It seems he had wandered away in mental derangement, and, had he died in this condition, and his body been found in the vicinity, it is difficult to conceive what could have saved the Trailors from the consequence of having murdered him. Or, if he had died, and his body never found, the case against them would have been quite as bad, for, although it is a principle of law that a conviction for murder shall not be had, unless the body of the deceased be discovered, it is to be remembered, that Henry testified that he saw Fisher's dead body.

BUMPED OFF IN THE BACKYARD

Sometime about ten o'clock on the night of May 15, 1856, George Anderson woke up and padded out of the bedroom, through the dining room and out into the backyard. He wore only the drawers and socks he'd been sleeping in, plus an overcoat he'd thrown on, perhaps for propriety's sake or perhaps to ward off the night chill. He might have been on his way to use the privy; he'd been sick to his stomach frequently over the past few weeks, and though he was starting to recover, he'd been feeling poorly that evening. Or he might have heard a noise and decided to investigate; he'd been told of a strange man lurking around his house lately and had taken to carrying a pistol for protection. He had the pistol with him now, in the pocket of his coat.

Whatever his reason for leaving the safety of his bed that fateful night, George Anderson didn't live to regret it. An hour later, he was discovered sprawled out across the backyard with a fractured skull, dead. A hammer, about the size and shape of the hole in Anderson's head, lay a few feet away in the grass.

Within a few minutes, as word of Anderson's demise spread, friends, neighbors, doctors and looky lous descended on the house, some to help and some to gawk. The body was moved indoors and examined by the doctors, who agreed that death had been caused, probably instantly, by the blow to the head. But Drs. Fowler and Lord, the Anderson family physicians, weren't content to let the matter lie there. Anderson's illness over the past several weeks had perplexed them; try as they might, they could not name the disease from which he suffered. In fact, they had started to question whether it had been a disease at all or if it might have been something more sinister. Dr. Fowler had begun to suspect strychnine poisoning and even taken it upon himself to capture and kill a stray cat with strychnine to observe the poison's effects. Chillingly, the dying creature's spasms resembled the agonies periodically suffered by Anderson while in the throes of his illness.

Now, with Anderson's body laid out on the sofa, the physicians couldn't help but wonder if someone had started out trying to poison him and just used a blunt instrument to finish the job. They decided that an impromptu autopsy was in order. The Andersons' sitting room seemed like as good a place as any to disembowel a corpse; so, over the hysterical protestations of Anderson's wife, they began. It was hard to concentrate with Jane Anderson carrying on like that in the next room, but eventually they got around to removing the stomach, where they found what they considered conclusive proof that Anderson had ingested strychnine.

The deputy sheriff, who had been prowling around collecting evidence, was informed of the possible strychnine twist. He was also formulating a theory as to who might be responsible. Acting on a hunch, he went to the house where Theodore Anderson boarded. Theodore, George's nephew, had lived with his now-dead uncle until the previous March, when George had abruptly asked him to find other accommodations. In the name of the law, the sheriff charged into the room Theodore now occupied and broke open a trunk labeled with his name. Inside was a picture of George's wife and a small vial of something that looked suspiciously like strychnine. Theodore Anderson was arrested immediately and charged with murder.

News of George Anderson's death and Theodore Anderson's arrest swept through the town like wildfire. Almost at once, the rumor mill began churning. The *Illinois State Journal* reported that there was no doubt Anderson's death was "a most foul murder" but would go no further, teasing its readers that while "there are a thousand rumors in circulation," it would print none of them "for fear of prejudicing the public mind." The *Daily Illinois Register* was almost as circumspect, declaring "as delicate domestic affairs are mingled up with this lamentable tragedy, we shall forbear to give further particulars until legal investigation has been had." Under the circumstances, even the coy mention of "delicate domestic affairs" might have been a shade too suggestive, for the town had already come to its own conclusion about the state of the Anderson household. Popular consensus held that Jane Anderson was having an affair with her husband's nephew, Theodore, and that both of them had conspired to poison and then bludgeon George to death.

When the case came before a grand jury in June, both Theodore and Jane Anderson were indicted for murder. The town was understandably horrified, for the whole situation was frightening on many different levels. George

Lincoln's second law partner, Stephen T. Logan, was one of the best defense attorneys in Springfield. *Courtesy of* History of Sangamon County, Illinois, *1881.*

Anderson had been killed on the way to his privy, for heaven's sake, right in his own backyard. It was terrifying to think that one might not survive the trip across one's own backyard, which everyone took several times a day. The idea that his wife had been engaged in hanky-panky with the boarder was terrifying, too. Lots of people took in boarders, and they were generally young, single, frisky men in the prime of their lives. Who knew what might go on between a virile boarder and a bored housewife when the husband was away at work?

The case went to trial in November 1856. The prosecuting attorneys were State's Attorney Amzi McWilliams, whom many people considered an ass (Judge David Davis later called him a "low vulgar man"), and Usher Linder, a legal pit bull with a reputation as a keen prosecutor. McWilliams had initially sought Abraham Lincoln's help in prosecuting the case, but Lincoln had turned him down. Lincoln ended up arguing for the defense, along with, it seemed, half the lawyers in town, including Lincoln's former partner Stephen T. Logan, newbie John T. Rosette, Lincoln's other former partner John T. Stuart, Lincoln's brother-in-law's brother Benjamin S. Edwards, Thomas Lewis and William Campbell.

The courtroom was packed with people eager to hear the salacious testimony of the most scandalous case Springfield had seen in years. They were not disappointed: witnesses went on at length about the position, dress and temperature of the body; of the nature of the wound; about Theodore's tendency to hang around and stare creepily at the Anderson house; about a tiff between George and Jane Anderson; about the time Jane had combed Theodore's hair before bed; about the symptoms and spasms George had suffered in his previous illness; and about the sound the saw made as it cut through George Anderson's skull during the autopsy. The prosecution painted a picture of two illicit lovers who had conspired to kill the cuckolded husband with strychnine, until the doctors became suspicious, and then had switched to blunt force trauma to finish the job. The defense maintained that Theodore had the strychnine only to treat a skin condition. It went out of its way to emphasize the happiness of the Andersons' marriage and Jane Anderson's sterling qualities as a wife and suggested that George Anderson might have fallen and hit his head during one of his "spasms" the night he died.

During the prosecution's closing arguments, Linder went for what he thought would be a home run. He called the jury's attention to the defendant, Theodore Anderson, who had been fooling around all trial, talking to the lawyers, looking at law books and generally not behaving with the solemnity expected during proceedings on which his life depended. "Gentlemen of the jury," Linder had thundered, "if you wanted any additional evidence of this man's guilt, it would only be necessary for you to recur to his boldness and impudence on this trial." It would have been an amazing point, if only Linder had known what he was talking about. Unfortunately, he didn't; the man he had pointed to hastily stood up and introduced himself as John Rosette, one of the attorneys for the defense, and everyone in the courtroom roared with laughter.

The trial ended at nine o'clock in the evening. It was three o'clock in the morning before the jury had reached its verdict: Theodore Anderson and Jane Anderson were found not guilty of murder.

Theodore Anderson eventually went back to New Jersey, from whence he had come. Jane Anderson stayed in Springfield. She didn't lose her taste for young male boarders, however. By 1860, she had two carpenters from New Jersey living with her and her four children in the house she had shared with George Anderson.

A SHOT IN THE DARK

On Friday, February 20, 1857, Walter Clark stopped in for a drink at the tavern John Bantzhouse kept in his home in New Berlin, just outside Springfield. History records little about the high-strung Mr. Bantzhouse, except that he kept a loaded shotgun at hand in his business, and nothing about the unfortunate Mr. Clark, except that he picked the wrong place to quench his thirst that night. By the end of the night, a blast from Bantzhouse's gun would leave Clark's entrails plastered all over the back wall of the tavern.

Details about what happened that night to set Bantzhouse off are vague. The Springfield newspaper reported only that he "became incensed at a party of men in his house, and in the melee the lights were extinguished." Old-timers from New Berlin later reminisced that Clark had scuffled with Bantzhouse and pushed him into a stove, severely burning his temper as well as his flesh. Whatever the cause, Bantzhouse's reaction was swift and vengeful. According to the newspaper, he "took his gun, which was loaded, and stepping outside, discharged the contents into the room through the window," killing Clark instantly. "The practice of keeping fire-arms loaded and ready for immediate use cannot be too severely reprehended," the editors concluded dourly.

Bantzhouse was arrested within a few days and indicted for murder. His case came before the Sangamon Circuit Court in early May but was continued to the fall term of court. When his case came up for trial again that August, Bantzhouse was ready, having armed himself with a crack defense team composed of former and future congressman John A. McClernand, Abraham Lincoln, Lincoln's partner William H. Herndon and Herndon's brother Elliot B. Herndon.

Lincoln immediately wrote a motion for a change of venue, arguing that his client would not be able to receive a fair trial in Sangamon County and requesting a move to Macoupin County instead. Requesting a change of venue was standard practice when the defendant was accused of murder or violent crime. It bought time, which always helped the defense, and it got the defendant away from an area where emotions, and biases, generally ran high.

Lincoln's move to Macoupin County might have been exceptionally shrewd, under the circumstances. In the mid-1850s, anti-immigrant sentiments in the United States were rampant, occasionally leading to riots or mob violence. The fastest-growing political party in the East was the rabidly nativist Know-Nothing Party, whose members feared that German and Irish Catholic immigrants were undermining American values. Lincoln, acutely aware that suspicion of Catholics and immigrants was widespread in Springfield, might have requested Macoupin County specifically for its large German population in the hopes that his German client might find a sympathetic jury among them.

But if the old-timers at New Berlin are to be believed, Lincoln planned to see that his client never came to trial at all. According to their stories, Lincoln told Bantzhouse that his case looked bad for him but that the indictment looked faulty and Lincoln thought he could get it quashed for

John Bantzhouse kept a tavern in his home and a shotgun close at hand. *Courtesy of* Illustrated Atlas Map of Sangamon County, Illinois; *Brink, McCormick, 1874.*

informality. (An indictment could be quashed, or overthrown, if the court found it irregular or defective in some way. This put the prosecution back to square one in terms of getting up a second indictment and bought the defense still more time.) Lincoln reportedly advised Bantzhouse to have a carriage and a fast team of horses ready and to bolt as soon as he received word that the indictment was quashed.

This is not the only anecdote of Lincoln advising his clients to make a getaway rather than face justice. In 1859, Melissa Goings was charged with murder after she had bashed in her husband's head with a piece of firewood. The old lout had it coming; he'd been beating Melissa for years, and she apparently decided that she'd had enough. The night he was killed, her husband had been trying to choke the life out of her. Melissa retained a sympathetic Lincoln as her defense attorney. When the day of her trial arrived, however, she failed to appear in court and was never heard from again. When the bailiff accused Lincoln of having encouraged his client to flee the state, there is a story that Lincoln replied, "She wanted to know where she could get a drink of water, and I told her there was mighty good water in Tennessee." There is no documentary evidence that Lincoln actually said such a thing, but there is evidence that Goings fled the state—county deed records later placed her in California.

We will never know if Bantzhouse really did flee on Lincoln's advice, but we do know that he really did flee. The indictment against him was indeed quashed, and Bantzhouse was discharged from custody under some technicality of the law. On October 6, 1857, the *Illinois State Journal* reported that "before another indictment could be framed, he had made use of leg-bail and taken to the woods," adding, dryly but accurately, that "it is probable that he will not be heard of very speedily in this part of the country."

INFANTICIDE OF AN ILLEGITIMATE CHILD

John and Elizabeth Broeckel thought that there was something strange about Maria from the very beginning. They had taken her into their house as a servant girl in November 1855. It was a gesture of pity, really—the girl was obviously poor and had no place else to go. She told them that she was from St. Louis; that she was an orphan and a widow; that her husband had died two weeks earlier and their house had burned down; and that she had given a doctor all the money she had and was penniless. The Broeckels had only meant to keep her until they could find a job for her in someone else's house, but when she broke down in tears and told them she was pregnant, they didn't have the heart to send her away, so she stayed until the baby was born. Maria named him James McCutcheon—after his late father, she explained. She always seemed like a good mother, and the child seemed like a healthy baby. Still, there was something not quite right about Maria.

And then, in June 1856, baby James McCutcheon was found dead along a country road south of Springfield. A handkerchief had been tied over his nose and mouth, and he had been smothered to death. Maria was the only suspect.

She went before a grand jury on November 18 and was charged with the murder of her infant son. On December 1, she appeared in the Sangamon County Circuit Court for her arraignment before the Honorable Abraham Lincoln, who was filling in on the bench for Judge David Davis, as he occasionally did when Davis was unwell. A note in the judge's docket in Lincoln's handwriting records that Maria entered a plea of not guilty, and Lincoln set a trial date for the following Monday, December 8. Maria would have to wait for more months for her day in court; a motion on the part of the defense resulted in a continuance until the spring term of court.

Finally, in April 1857, her case went to trial. Maria's plea of not guilty was by reason of insanity. This was probably a wise move; as witness after witness came to the stand to testify, the story Maria had concocted about her life quickly began to unravel, indicating that she was either an accomplished liar or, as she claimed, insane.

Her name, it turned out, was Maria House, not Maria McCutcheon. She was not an orphan. She was not from St. Louis. It was true that she had been married, but her husband had died three years ago, and his name was not James McCutcheon. Before coming to the Broeckels, she had worked for about a year as a servant in the house of Hiram Alexander and his wife, where she was in the habit of drinking large quantities of camphor. This made her, in the words of one witness, "exhibit symptoms of derangement of the mind."

Springfield's accused murderers came to trial before Judge David Davis, who presided over the Sangamon County Circuit Court from 1848 to 1862. *Courtesy of Library of Congress, Prints and Photographs Division.*

She had also been sleeping with Hiram Alexander, who was the father of her baby.

Things were not looking good for Maria's case. She had been caught in several lies, found out as the mother of an illegitimate child and tagged with suggestions of substance abuse. The deceased baby had last been seen alive in her arms not far from the place where its body was eventually found.

To make matters worse, halfway through the trial a pair of thieves almost broke out of the county jail. They picked the lock with a pair of scissors and succeeded in throwing the bolt before the jailor's sons overheard them and stymied their attempt. Maria House supplied them with the scissors.

The defense was left with the distasteful, but sadly not difficult, task of painting Maria as a crazy person.

The first defense witness, William Wardall, started off gamely enough, testifying that Maria had told him that her name was Louisa and that from her odd behavior he had "formed the opinion that she was not in her right mind," though it might have been overkill when he wound up his testimony by saying, "I would not have trusted her with my children on account of her want of capacity."

Sarah Condell, whose sister had once employed Maria in her house, had no trouble elaborating on Maria's want of capacity. She recalled a time when her sister was away, and Maria had been left in charge of the house under Sarah's supervision. Sarah had wandered into a room only to find Maria attempting to build a fire using pieces of wood so long that they jutted out from the fireplace and onto the floor, around which she had piled wooden shingles for good measure. Certain that she had just saved the house from a conflagration, Sarah ushered Maria outside and was on her way out herself when she noticed Maria double back and reenter the house. Sarah found her curled in a small, dark closet where she declared she intended to spend the night. Once more Sarah kicked her out, this time taking Maria with her to her brother's house. Maria griped and whined every step of the way about how she preferred to sleep in the closet.

Two more witnesses took the stand, helpfully adding that Maria, to them, seemed "insane," "not in her right mind" and "unbalanced," and then her father and sister were called to drive the point home. Maria, they explained, had fallen ill with fever ten or fifteen years ago after a trip to Iowa and ever since then had occasionally experienced "spells" lasting two or three hours during which "her eyes looked wild and wavered" and she appeared insensible, sometimes muttering to herself, sometimes saying nothing.

If they had sold their daughter and sister down the river as a loony, it was for a good cause, for when the prosecution recalled Dr. E.S. Fowler on the last day of testimony, he declared that "from testimony of witnesses I think the prisoner is a fitter subject for an insane hospital than a jail; I don't think she is morally an accountable being, she seems from early infancy to have been weak-minded." He added, pointedly, "I should say from her appearance that she has imbecile mind; I think there are others in the room with minds as imbecile as hers, who are free agents."

With that ringing endorsement of Maria's claim to liberty, the testimony was closed. Surprisingly little had been disclosed about the circumstances of the baby's death—only that Maria had been seen holding him near the train depot the night before and that the next morning the body was found on a country road. There seemed to be a tacit understanding that Maria had been the one who had smothered him; really, there were no other suspects, no other people with possible motives. So the question was, had she killed him with malice aforethought? Or had she been suffering one of her "spells"?

After the attorneys made their closing arguments, the jury deliberated for two hours before returning with a verdict: not guilty. Maria House went home and promptly disappeared from all further historical record.

A DANCE TURNS DEADLY

Winter was a lively time in Springfield. For the town's social elite, it meant a time of balls and receptions to entertain the state legislature, whose arrival for the winter session gave the town a bustling, festive air. For the country folk, winter was a time to celebrate a successful harvest and a lull in farm work with dances and sleigh rides fueled by homemade spirits. People from all walks of life looked forward to the social gatherings that filled the long, dark evening hours with the expectation of good friends, good food and good cheer.

For Richard Whitehead, the party he went to on January 17, 1860, would be his last.

It was held at Joseph Newland's house on Lick Creek. The house wasn't very big—only two rooms—and both of the rooms were filled to the brim with people dancing and laughing. Whitehead, though, wasn't in a laughing mood. He had heard that George Pulliam would be at this party, and Pulliam rubbed him the wrong way. Whitehead had been itching to take a swing at him for weeks. And not just with his fists; no, he wanted to take a crack at Pulliam with a small weight fastened to a leather strap called a slung shot, a weapon designed to do grievous damage when used for striking.

He'd almost had his chance at a dance a month earlier. He'd gone to a party armed with a borrowed slung shot and ready for trouble. James Mann had come up to him, flushed and happy with dancing and drink and jovially remarked that the ball was going off in very good style.

"If I can get a chance at a certain man here, the ball will not go off as well as it is going now," Whitehead replied. He showed Mann his slung shot and vowed that he would use it on Pulliam and said that he did not care how much it hurt him. Mann, catching on that his companion was rather short on holiday cheer that evening, backed away. Later, Mann pulled Pulliam aside and told him to be on his guard. In the meantime, Whitehead, unaware of any possible breach of etiquette incurred by bringing weapons to a Christmas party, blithely repeated his threat to several more people.

Whitehead had missed his chance that time, but ever since he'd taken the slung shot everywhere, ready for any opportunity to lay into his nemesis. He had it with him this evening, at Newland's dancing party, and was sure that he'd get his chance before the night was over.

He was not the only one in a fighting mood at the dance. The host, Joseph Newland, was irritated with Benjamin Haskett over a bill of fare that Haskett had never settled up. Newland cornered Haskett in the smaller of the two rooms and vented his spleen. The argument might have escalated right then and there had Pulliam not stepped forward and played peacemaker, frontier-style, by negotiating a truce that called for the two men to settle their differences in a good, old-fashioned fistfight the next day.

All parties seemed content—until Whitehead charged in. "Newland, stand up for your rights, and if you are not able to take your part, I will help you," he bellowed, crowding in between the two men.

"Now, now," Pulliam said. "It is only a small fuss—the boys are now satisfied, and they have agreed to fight the thing out tomorrow."

Enraged, Whitehead swung on Pulliam. "You're the cause of this fuss, George!"

Pulliam, whose peacemaking tendencies were severely tested in the presence of this oaf, snapped back, "Oh, shut up, you have no right to butt in here."

"I'll say what I please!" Whitehead roared. "*You* shut up, this whole thing is your fault!"

Pulliam was at the end of his patience. "You are a damned liar!" he yelled.

It was like pouring gasoline on an open flame. Suddenly, Whitehead lunged forward and whapped Pulliam on the head with his slung shot, a nasty blow that would later swell to an egg-shaped knot.

Accused murderers such as George Pulliam often languished in jail for months before going to trial. *Courtesy of* Frank Leslie's Illustrated Newspaper, *July 22 1865.*

His victory was short-lived. Pulliam, with reflexes like a cat, quickly struck back: three blows, in rapid succession. And Pulliam was holding a bowie knife.

The first two blows were glancing cuts to the face, but the third one found its mark: the knife penetrated between the first and second ribs, slicing its way downward before finally piercing the heart and lungs. Whitehead backed off and took six or eight steps forward before collapsing. Within a few minutes, he was dead.

Pulliam was arrested two days later at his uncle's house four miles distant. He did not resist but went peaceably to jail, remarking that he could have escaped long before had he felt so disposed.

He had to wait for nearly four months before he was given a trial, although this delay worked to his advantage, as it gave the townsfolk time to cool their heads over the matter. Even so, more than one hundred people were interviewed for the jury before reasonably unbiased men could be found.

The trial began on Thursday, May 10. Pulliam's lawyers were Stephen T. Logan (formerly Abraham Lincoln's law partner and widely reputed to be the best defense attorney in town), James Matheny (the best man at Lincoln's wedding), George Shutt, James B. White and John E. Rosette. Lincoln's current law partner, William H. Herndon, appeared for the prosecution. The stakes were high. If Pulliam was convicted of murder, he'd be sentenced to hang.

Pulliam pleaded "not guilty." Over the course of three days, testimony was heard that suggested that Whitehead was less the innocent victim and more a hothead with a slung shot who had been looking for trouble. Still, Pulliam *had* plunged a bowie knife into his heart. On Saturday night, the verdict was rendered: George Pulliam was found guilty of the lesser charge of manslaughter and sentenced to seven years in the state penitentiary in Joliet.

A week later, the prosecuting attorney's law partner was nominated as the Republican candidate for president of the United States.

Chapter 7

CIVIL WAR SHENANIGANS

Abraham Lincoln was elected president of the United States on November 6, 1860. In February of the next year, he left Springfield for good, bound for Washington, D.C., and the momentous task of holding together a nation that seemed determined to rend itself in two. Little more than a month after he had taken office, the shots fired on Fort Sumter signaled the start of the Civil War. The country would never be the same.

Springfield would never be the same, either. The once-sleepy prairie town was transformed within a matter of months to a bustling hub of military activity. In April 1861, Ulysses S. Grant arrived to muster and drill troops at Camp Yates, the military training facility on the west side of town. As much as the citizens of Springfield might have supported the troops, they did not support having them quartered within city limits, where soldiers were known to steal fruit from orchards and chickens from pens and often cause trouble while drunk. A new military camp was called for, and in August 1861 General William Tecumseh Sherman arrived in Springfield with orders to select an appropriate location. With the help of the state's treasurer, William Butler, Sherman chose a cool, shady clearing on the banks of Clear Lake, six miles northeast of Springfield. It was named Camp Butler, in William Butler's honor.

Within days, troops began pouring into the new camp. By August 9 the population numbered 1,500 men. By August 21 there were 5,000 men in camp, with hundreds more arriving daily. The camp expanded to accommodate its growing numbers, but the men were still quartered too close for comfort.

Six miles northwest of Springfield, Camp Butler served as a Civil War training facility and housed prisoners of war. *Courtesy of Paul Angle's* Here I Have Lived: A History of Lincoln's Springfield, *1935.*

Crowded and unsanitary conditions bred diseases that swept through the tightly packed inhabitants like wildfire. Things only grew worse when the first shipment of Confederate prisoners arrived after the Battle of Fort Donelson in February 1862. By March of that year, ill soldiers were dying at a rate of 3 or 4 per day. By June more than 300 men had been hospitalized, suffering from the ravages of typhoid, dysentery, pneumonia and smallpox.

Aside from sickness, the soldiers' worst enemy was boredom. Drills started at 5:30 a.m. and went on until dark: endless marching and maneuvering, often carrying sticks in place of muskets, which were hard to come by in sufficient numbers. When the soldiers weren't drilling, they were engaged in equally mundane tasks such as digging ditches, gathering firewood and building roads and barracks. It was enough to drive a man to drink, though hard liquor was forbidden on camp premises.

The result was that Camp Butler teemed with thousands of men who were alternately bored, lonely, exhausted and ornery, men who were always looking for a bit of distraction from the monotony of camp life. Springfield was an alluring outlet for their energies, bursting as it was with the bars and brothels that had sprung up to meet the demands of these frisky soldiers, with its shops and businesses where jangling pay might be parted with, with its belles and beauties who swooned at the sight of a uniform. Most of the time, they behaved themselves in town. Often enough, however, they did not, and the newspapers started printing lengthy police reports of drunkenness, prostitution and gambling along with dispatches from the front lines of battles. What follows is a sampling of some of Springfield's most talked about Civil War shenanigans.

REVELRY AND RIOTS

Every so often, the soldiers at Camp Butler liked to go out and raise a little hell to escape from the boredom of life in camp, with its endless drills, its endless time spent sitting around and its endless deprivation of female company. These young men had joined the army for adventure. If camp life couldn't provide them excitement, they would strike out at night and stir up a little of their own. And wherever a group of intoxicated soldiers gathered, there was bound to be trouble.

It was rare that a week went by in Springfield without some ruckus caused by drunk soldiers who had sneaked away without clearance. Some of the townspeople were starting to get fed up. There were rumblings of threats to take the law into their own hands if officers couldn't keep a better handle on their soldiers. Right now it seemed as though they were out of control. Sure, hard alcohol was forbidden in camp, and they weren't supposed to leave without written permission, but after evening roll call, surveillance was laughably light; for all intents and purposes, the soldiers were largely unmonitored until the following morning. And while there were a few sentinels posted at the camp's perimeter, it wasn't hard to bribe them or fool them with fake passes.

Just before eleven o'clock on the night of October 8, 1861, a party of six men from Captain Trafton's company, attached to the Seventh Cavalry Regiment, left the camp in search of a good time. Little did they know that their evening would quickly spiral out of control, leaving one of their number dead and another barely clinging to life. They had used forged passes to slip past guards who were unable or unwilling to see that the six soldiers were already visibly drunk and obviously intended to get drunker before the night was over. Stumbling, singing and slurring their words, the happy group lurched its way northward. Soon they came to the house where Andrew Young, a fifty-year-old German farmer, lived with his wife and five small children.

What happened next was a blur of violence and chaos. Young and his wife gave the police a broken account of what transpired. Four of the men had dragged Mrs. Young out of the house and threw her onto a nearby pile of straw, where each of them then took turns raping her. The other two men had torn up the house, first flinging mugs and glasses at Andrew and then shooting at him with their pistols. When they started after his thirteen-year-old daughter, Lena, who was lying in the parlor recovering from a lingering illness, Andrew could take no more. He seized a billet of firewood and struck one of the soldiers across the temple with it, killing him instantly; then he beat the other soldier nearly to death. The four soldiers who had raped Mrs. Young fled into the night, sending help back to the house for their severely wounded comrade.

This report was published in the newspaper, sparking outcry and outrage among the citizens of Springfield. As it turned out, however, it wasn't entirely accurate. The next day, Captain Trafton wrote a letter to the editor of the newspaper to set the record straight.

It seemed that the soldiers hadn't randomly stumbled on Andrew Young's house. They had set out for the place deliberately, knowing—as did everyone at Camp Butler—that Young ran a tavern and whorehouse out of his home, selling the soldiers whiskey and the use of his wife for a modest fee. Young had frequently been seen out near the camp, trying to entice soldiers to visit his house, where they might satisfy their animal desires with his wife and get drunk on his liquor.

What happened the night before hadn't been a random act of violence perpetrated on an innocent family, Trafton wrote. It was merely revelry gone awry at a place that encouraged and facilitated drinking and fornication. Mrs. Young hadn't been gang raped; her services had been bought by the four soldiers with the full knowledge and consent of her husband. The soldiers hadn't flung mugs and glasses and shot their pistols with the intent to harm Young or distract him from what was happening with his wife; it was just a drunken spree that had gotten out of control. And Trafton insisted that it was a bald-faced lie that the soldiers had attempted to violate the person of thirteen-year-old Lena Young. Why would they do that when Mrs. Young's services were readily offered? Grafton's men had used poor judgment when they snuck away from Camp Butler to go drinking and carousing, Grafton acknowledged, but that was all. He wanted the truth to be known and their reputations cleared of the stain of being "violators of the sanctity of a respectable home." There was nothing respectable about Andrew Young and his wife. Failure to realize this had gotten one of his men killed and another one beaten within an inch of his life.

Civil War soldiers generally couldn't stand the camp sutler. The sutler wasn't a soldier himself, but he made his money off enlisted men. He was the person who sold everything, from razors to shoes, stationery and coffee. His goods were usually shoddy, and his prices were usually high, but his customers put up with him because he was the only game in town, holder of a monopoly on the sale of nonmilitary merchandise in camp.

The soldiers at Camp Butler had even more reason to be suspicious of their sutler—James C. Hall had been born in North Carolina. Overcharging the poor boys in blue for their little luxuries was just about as much as you could expect from a Southerner. Under the best of circumstances, they tolerated him, grudgingly. But when Hall dared to tangle with a drunk soldier, the camp's outraged response quickly escalated into a riot that left outhouses overturned and Hall bruised and bloodied.

The trouble all started with the soldier, who wasn't even a soldier in good standing but rather a deserter captured near Chicago and brought to Camp Butler for disciplinary action. This man ambled into Hall's store on April 27, 1863, called for two glasses of cider, drank them and ambled out again without paying. When he got thirsty again, he returned to Hall's store and asked for more cider. Hall may have been a Southerner and a sutler, but he was nobody's fool, and the request was this time refused.

This is when things got ugly.

The soldier, as the newspaper reported, "commenced abusing Mr. Hall in the most dastardly manner." Not content with merely yelling and swearing at the bewildered sutler, he also took a swing at him. But Hall, as previously noted, was nobody's fool, and he was no more willing to be hit than he was to be ripped off. Ducking the blow, he picked up a four-pound weight from the counter and bashed the deserter on the head with it, laying him out flat.

It was actually an impressive display of reflexes, but the crowd of soldiers gathered outside didn't see it that way. All they saw was that a dirty, thieving Rebel sutler had brained one of their comrades, nevermind the fact that this comrade was a deserter and had thrown the first punch. They hovered around the door of Hall's store and would have charged in and dragged him out had not the camp's commanding officer dispersed them.

Only temporarily deterred from their vengeance, they were back at nightfall, this time several hundred strong and armed with kerosene and kindling, intent on burning the store to the ground. Before they could drop the match, however, they were halted by the news that the building did not belong to Hall. Their momentary disappointment turned to violent glee when Hall came out of the store, and assault and battery replaced arson on the evening's agenda. The sutler was knocked down and kicked in the side, chest and face, probably by the very boots he had sold. He only escaped when the evening drumroll sounded, briefly distracting the mob from its violent work. Without Hall underfoot to receive their punishment, the rioters were forced to vent their anger on the camp's enclosure, which they stripped of its boards, and the hospital's outhouses, which they knocked over.

The party came to a quick and disappointing end when a handful of officers showed up with a detachment of troops to quell the riot and restore the peace. Hall limped home to nurse his injuries and, probably, to reconsider his line of work, and the rioting soldiers were arrested and court-martialed.

On February 14, 1864, the citizens of Springfield were in a high state of excitement. But it wasn't love that caused their hearts to race this chilly Valentine's Day afternoon; it was the news, spreading quickly through town, that a gang of soldiers was rampaging through the business district. The rumors flew fast and furious: They tore up saloons! A man was killed! Pistol shots fired! One soldier turned on his comrades with a musket! The mayor was desperate to quell the riot!

Six unruly soldiers were the source of the disturbance. They were drunk, of course—the seeds of the kind of trouble they were causing don't germinate in a sober mind—and their primary mission seemed to be the destruction of several downtown saloons. First they had gone into Corcoran & Cavanaugh's and called for a bottle of whiskey, though it turned out they were less interested in the contents of the bottle than the bottle itself. As soon as it was set down before them, they picked it up and heaved it against the mirror behind the bar. Bottles, glasses, pitchers and decanters followed, until the saloon looked like the inside of a snow globe with shards of glass in place of confetti snow. George Whalen of the Twenty-sixth Illinois tried to stop them (he not being a member of the demolition club) and received a bowie knife to the forehead for his efforts.

Having smashed up Corcoran & Cavanaugh's to their satisfaction, they moved on to Loeb's saloon on Jefferson Street and repeated the process from start to finish, beginning with the call for whiskey and ending with the destruction of anything within reach. This time, they threw a chair at the bartender for good measure, though he was a harder target to hit than the wall and mirror and thereby escaped unscathed. The same could not be said for his bar, which was littered with fragments of glass and wood that only minutes before had been bottles and chairs.

Another soldier tried to join the unruly bunch on their way to the Chenery House, but his company was unwelcome, a sentiment they expressed by beating him off with palings torn from a nearby fence. Being unable to join them, this unhappy fellow decided to beat them. He ran ahead to the Chenery House and grabbed a musket (apparently hotels in those days had muskets lying around) and met them at the door. Firing recklessly, he managed to drive them several feet back before one of the cleverer fellows noticed that the musket was not loaded. Emboldened in the face of an impotent weapon, the rowdy group surged forward and pushed its way into the hotel's office.

They only managed to break the glass out of one door before the provost marshal showed up and put a quick stop to their fun. The two most inebriated members of the group were put under arrest, the other four fled back to camp and the rest of Springfield's saloons tentatively cracked open their blinds and doors and made themselves ready for the next wave of customers.

AN OFFICER WITH A HAIR-TRIGGER TEMPER

Captain Neussell, of the Eighty-second Illinois Regiment, Company G, liked his liquor. He wasn't alone; a good chunk of many soldiers' pay disappeared into the pockets of Springfield's saloonkeepers every month, and Springfielders were quickly becoming used to the sight of drunk, off-duty soldiers roaming around their streets at night. The trouble with Captain Neussell was that he didn't confine his drinking to nighttime. He didn't even wait until he was off-duty. He was an officer with a hair-trigger temper, a sidearm and a habit of reporting for duty while intoxicated. It was a dangerous combination.

Thomas Vines learned this the hard way on November 3, 1862.

The day had started out like any other. Vines, a teamster employed by the U.S. quartermasters' department at Camp Butler, had received word that Colonel Hecker's regiment was under marching orders and would be departing Springfield. Vines was instructed to transport the regiment's baggage from camp to the railroad depot. It was heavy and tedious work, but Vines was young and strong and good with his team.

His first piece of bad luck befell him as he was hefting the first load of baggage onto his cart. One of the soldiers—either accidentally or on purpose, no one was sure—poked the flank of one of Vines's mules with his bayonet, causing the beast to take fright and bolt, charging through the lines of soldiers assembled and running some distance before Vines regained control of his team. Upon returning to Camp Butler after dropping off the first load of baggage, Vines found himself under arrest for having run through the lines. Indignant, Vines explained the circumstances that had caused his mules to bolt, and the arresting officer relented and released him.

He was on his way to pick up a second load of baggage at about one o'clock that afternoon when Captain Neussell, smelling of drink and looking for a fight, wobbled up to his wagon and attempted to arrest him a second time. When Vines balked, insisting that he had already been arrested and released and was now free to resume his work, Neussell gritted his teeth and tried to forcibly pull Vines out of his saddle. Vines held his ground, resisting Neussell's grasping hands. The two men scuffled a bit, but Vines was a good horseman and steady in his saddle, while Neussell was intoxicated and unsteady on his feet. Vines succeeded in pushing Neussell away from him. Neussell, stumbling back, lost his footing, tumbled to the ground and was promptly run over by Vines's wagon.

This was Vines's second, and final, piece of bad luck. Neussell's body was bruised but his pride was in tatters—scores of soldiers milling around had seen his ignominious fall and impersonation of a human speed bump. He struggled to his feet, red-faced with anger.

"Shoot the damned rascal!" he yelled.

No sooner had he spoken than half a dozen pistols were drawn and cocked. The crack of gunshots filled the air, over and over again, each man firing several rounds. The team of mules, frightened by the noise, bolted for the second time that day.

When the smoke cleared, Vines was slumped on the ground, killed instantly by a bullet through the neck. Two more soldiers were badly injured, having been run over by the wagon when the team charged away. And one of the mules was dying of two gunshot wounds to the side.

The coroner and commander of the post ruled Vines's death an unprovoked murder. All six officers involved, including the often-intoxicated Captain Neussell, were arrested for the crime.

SHOT BY A SOLDIER IN THE STREET

The Pilcher kids had been troublemakers for as long as anyone in Springfield could remember. The old man, Moses, did what he could to rein them in, but ever since his wife died he'd had his hands full trying to handle all seven of them by himself. It was easier in the winter when the carpentry business slowed down some, and he had more time on his hands, but he'd never quite managed to have the time to raise them up civilized, like his wife would have wanted.

Oh, the girls were all right. Lucinda, the eldest, was a big help, but even with her gentle influence the boys still ran wild. Jeptha wasn't sixteen years old the first time he got caught stealing, and he kept it up through his teenage years, even after he'd been caught and hauled into court, twice. As Wesley and John got older, they followed in their older brother's drinking and thieving footsteps, despite their father's best efforts to teach them the carpenter's trade and give them a dose of responsibility. Although they managed to learn enough about the trade to get some work here and there, their main occupations seemed to be drinking and alternately bumming around and raising hell. It embarrassed Moses, a respectable, hardworking man who'd been chosen to serve on juries and even, back in '52, as a delegate to the Democratic Convention.

Wesley, the middle boy, seemed to be the worst of the bunch. When he was seventeen, he had assaulted a man and been indicted for attempted murder. It was probably only his youth that got him off the hook, but he sure didn't learn anything from his brush with the law. Since then he'd been arrested for cavorting with a prostitute, for breaking into a railroad car and two more times for assault and battery. When the war came, many young men of his age joined the service and marched off in defense of the Union. Wesley stayed in Springfield and wandered around in search of a drink or an item of value to filch. By 1863, he was known around town as a rowdy, a loafer and a thief.

St. Patrick's Day 1863 found Wesley downtown at the Milwaukee Beer Saloon with his brother and several of their roustabout friends, getting

Wesley Pilcher went for an ill-fated joyride on a dray cart on this corner on March 17, 1863. *Courtesy of* Illustrated Atlas Map of Sangamon County, Illinois; *Brink, McCormick, 1874.*

progressively more intoxicated as the morning melted into early afternoon. He wasn't Irish, but he and his cronies appreciated any reason to drink in the middle of the day. By about two o'clock, he was good and sauced and ready to stumble out in search of a little fun.

Lo and behold, he found fun parked right in front of the saloon in the form of an unattended dray cart hitched to a single taciturn mule. Wesley looked around, but the drayman was nowhere to be found. In his alcohol-soaked mind, one coherent thought floated forward: it was a good day for a joyride.

Giddy with mischief, Wesley hopped up onto the dray cart and gave the mule a nudge, sending it skittering across the road. His joy was short-lived; William O'Hara, the drayman, saw his cart go clattering down the street and took off after it. After grabbing the lines and bringing the mule to a halt, O'Hara wheeled on Wesley and demanded to know just what the hell he thought he was doing.

Truthfully, Wesley hadn't been thinking much at all. His synapses were firing even more slowly than usual through the boozy fog in his brain, and right now the only thing he knew for sure was that he didn't like the way that O'Hara was yelling at him. If only there was some way to shut him up…and then his bleary gaze fell on the iron pin that fastened the back of the dray cart. Lurching forward, Wesley grasped the iron pin, raised it high in the air and brought it crashing down on O'Hara's head.

His plan backfired. Rather than shutting him up, the blow caused O'Hara to howl like a banshee. O'Hara staggered around a little, grasping the wheel of his cart for support, and when his gingerly probing fingers found a deep, jagged, profusely bleeding gash on his forehead, he yelled even louder—this time for the police.

Wesley, annoyed with all the ruckus, stumbled over to the doorway of Spath's saloon and sat down next to his brother, absently picking at his fingernails with his pocketknife while a crowd of curious onlookers gathered to see what the fuss was about.

One of the people who heard the commotion was Emory P. Dustan, a twenty-five-year-old second lieutenant in the Fifty-eighth Illinois Regiment of Volunteers stationed at Camp Butler. He had been in Springfield since the previous night, rounding up deserters from boardinghouses and billiard parlors to take them back to camp. Hearing O'Hara's calls for the police, he left two of his prizes in the care of a fellow officer and jogged forward to investigate the disturbance and see if he could lend a hand.

Seeing the gaping wound on O'Hara's head, Dustan quickly scanned the crowd for the culprit. "Show me the person that struck you," he said to O'Hara. The injured drayman pointed to Wesley, still lounging in the doorway of the saloon. The crowd, whose number had grown to better than fifty at this point, yelled their encouragement: "That's right, arrest him!" Dustan, annoyed, yelled back, "If you want me to arrest him, why don't you help me do it?"

He approached Wesley cautiously, pistol drawn, and told him that he was placing him under arrest until the police arrived. Wesley, whose generally quarrelsome attitude was only exacerbated by drink, would have none of it.

"You have no authority to arrest me!" he roared. "I'll be goddamned if I let you take me!"

No stranger when it came to assault, Wesley charged forward and tried to strike Dustan with his fists. The officer, now blanched and perhaps wishing that he'd never interfered in the first place, held him off with his left hand and kept his pistol trained on him with his right.

"Stay back," Dustan warned. "Don't strike me or I'll shoot you."

But Wesley, drunk and belligerent, didn't know when to quit. He pushed forward, fists doubled, a menacing gleam in his glassy eyes, backing Dustan off the curb and into the street.

A second time Dustan issued his warning: "Stop, or I will shoot you." But Wesley kept advancing, aggressive, threatening, fists still raised in a fighting stance, and Dustan kept backing away, warily, pistol cocked.

The officer tried one more time: "Stay right there. I will shoot you." Wesley, probably figuring that Dustan was bluffing, pushed forward.

Dustan wasn't bluffing. Out of patience, and nearly out of space to retreat, he fired his weapon. The bullet struck Wesley in the neck, and he collapsed on the street, blood pouring from his mouth and nose. He died within minutes.

If his wayward brothers were affected by his death, they gave no outward sign of it. Three days later, John and Jeptha were arrested for robbery and spent the next six months in jail. Dustan, too, was arrested and court-martialed for killing Pilcher but was acquitted of all charges.

LINCOLN'S WARTIME NEPOTISM GONE BAD

When Abraham Lincoln first came to Springfield in 1837, he was, as Ninian Edwards would later describe him, "a mighty rough man," lacking the money and manners required for admission into polite society. Even so, Edwards, son of an Illinois governor and already an established legislator and lawyer, saw something promising in Lincoln and took him under his wing. Over the next four years, Lincoln was a frequent guest at Edwards's mansion on Aristocracy Hill, where he rubbed elbows with Springfield's social and political elite over elegant dinners served on crystal and china. On November 4, 1842, Lincoln became Edwards's brother-in-law when he married Mary Todd, sister of Edwards's wife, Elizabeth.

By 1860, their fortunes had reversed. Lincoln was now being talked of as a candidate for president of the United States, and Edwards was broke. Tail between his legs, Edwards came crawling to Lincoln for a loan of $1,500 in April of that year. Massive debt was not enough to curb Edwards's profligate spending, however, and by December he had shelled out $14,000 to build a house for his daughter and buy a newspaper for her husband. Deeper in the hole than ever (or, as Edwards put it, financially "much embarrassed"), he asked Lincoln for money a second time.

By June 1861, Edwards had slipped from financial embarrassment to financial ruin, or so he claimed, and Lincoln had been elected and sworn in as president of the United States. Despite the fact that he had campaigned for Stephen Douglas against Lincoln, Edwards was not above asking his powerful brother-in-law for a government job. Lincoln dragged his feet for a while but eventually capitulated and appointed Edwards commissary of subsistence with the rank of captain in the army. Edwards would be in charge of awarding contracts to provision the soldiers and prisoners of war at Springfield's nearby Camp Butler. Done honestly, Edwards's job would procure the best-quality rations and supplies at the lowest cost to the government. Done dishonestly, Edwards's job would line his own pockets and those of his cronies while leaving the soldiers with shoddy requisitions.

As soon as news of the forthcoming appointment reached Springfield, a howl of protest arose among its leading Republicans, who were sure that Edwards would favor fellow Democrats—or worse—with his contracts. Lincoln's inbox was flooded with angry letters from friends back home begging him to reconsider. While Edwards himself was not corrupt, they conceded, he was deeply entangled with a number of unsavory characters, chief among them the disgraced former governor Joel Matteson. "If appointed we feel assured that he may be an instrument only, in the hands of these men, with Gov Matteson at their head," wrote the Illinois secretary of state, state treasurer and state auditor.

Perhaps against his better judgment, Lincoln ignored these warnings and went forward with the appointment, repaying his brother-in-law's early kindnesses with the benefit of the doubt. Within three months, Edwards was indeed awarding contracts to Governor Matteson. Springfield's leading men were outraged that the man who had defrauded the state of nearly $250,000 was now personally furnishing supplies to the soldiers at Camp Butler. They wrote to Lincoln a second time, demanding Edwards's reassignment: "We protest that Mr Edwards is not, or ought not to be permitted to make such contracts, and we respectfully ask that he be assigned to duty, elsewhere, and be required to contract directly with honest men, and not indirectly with thieves and scoundrels."

Once again, Lincoln was torn between loyalty to his Republican friends in Springfield and loyalty to his kin, and once again he gave Edwards the benefit of the doubt. Edwards assured him that he had awarded contracts strictly to the lowest bidder and that he could not help the fact that one of the lowest bidders happened to be Governor Matteson's son-in-law. He kept his post, and for the next two years Lincoln heard little of his dealings in Springfield.

In this case, no news was not good news. By 1863, Lincoln's Republican friends were writing him again, complaining that Edwards, along with his crony William Bailhache, was using his office to fatten his own bank account. William Yates, a Springfield merchant, pointed out that two years earlier Edwards had been teetering on the verge of financial collapse, "and now I am told he brags on how much money he has made, has bought a fine Carriage & horses. And has large deposits in Bank. And all from a Salary of Eighteen hundred dollars as he told me himself." Yates could not account for the change in Edwards's fortunes; surely he must be getting kickbacks from his contracts. Worse, Edwards was handing out lucrative government contracts to people hostile to Lincoln and the Union: "I am told the Contracts have been given in almost every instance to parties who are thought to be Rebel Sympathizers. And who are known to be Blatant Democrats. And who exercise all their influence against your administration." Jacob Bunn, another Springfield merchant, concurred. Thanks to Edwards,

> *there are men here having no sympathy with your administration, who have not only been living off of the General Goverment for the past two years but getting rich from the stealings; (the sums acquired are too large to have been obtained honestly), who lose no opportunity to revile and denounce your administration; and whose pecuniary interest is not to put down the rebellion but to prolong it, in order to make more money.*

Edwards, aware that his townsmen were once again clamoring for his head, wrote to Lincoln, swearing up and down that he had done his job "conscientiously, faithfully and honestly, and without showing favor to any one" and reminding him of all the ways he had helped the president out over the years.

Lincoln, however, had had enough. He was an extremely patient man, but even he had limits to his forbearance. As he explained in a letter to Edwards's son-in-law:

> *Springfield is my home, and there, more than elsewhere, are my life-long friends. These, for now nearly two years, have been harrassing me because of Mr. E. & Mr. B. I think Mr. E. & Mr. B. without dishonesty on the other hand, could have saved me from this, if they had cared to do so. They have seemed to think that if they could keep their official record dryly correct, to say the least, it was not any difference*

how much they might provoke my friends, and harrass me. If this is too strong a statement of the case, still the result has been the same to me; and, as a misfortune merely, I think I have already borne a fair share of it.

He removed Edwards from office at the end of June.

Edwards never forgot the slight. After Lincoln was killed, William Herndon sat down to interview Edwards on his impressions of his famous brother-in-law.

"Lincoln was not a warm hearted man," Edwards told him. "[He] seemed to be ungrateful."

EPILOGUE

Abraham Lincoln returned to Springfield for the final time on May 3, 1865. It had been nearly three weeks since John Wilkes Booth's bullet felled him at the pinnacle of his presidency and nearly four years since he said goodbye to Springfield for the last time in his life. The entire town turned out to welcome him home—friends, family, clients and merchants, as well as people whom he had nodded to on the street—plus thousands more who poured in from all over the state to be there when the funeral train arrived.

Springfield had been preparing for the arrival of Lincoln's body for weeks. The entire downtown, as well as Lincoln's house, was swathed in black bunting. The Hall of Representatives—draped in black, with "sooner than surrender these principles, I would be assassinated on the spot" emblazoned around the cornice—was transformed into a funereal shrine. A spectacular gold, silver and crystal hearse was loaned from St. Louis. The following day was to be the last, grandest and most poignant of the twelve blockbuster funerals held at intervals along the train's route west, and at its close Lincoln's body would finally be laid to rest.

Notwithstanding this spectacular and expensive public outpouring of grief, the city of Springfield came within a hair of losing the privilege of keeping Lincoln's earthly remains for good. Mary, Lincoln's widow, initially wavered on the idea of burying Lincoln in Springfield, musing that perhaps Chicago or Washington, D.C., would be more appropriate. Prevailed upon by the current governor of Illinois, Richard Oglesby, and his immediate past

When Lincoln's body arrived in Springfield on May 3, 1865, practically every building in town was draped in black mourning crepe. *Courtesy of Sangamon Valley Collection, Lincoln Library, Springfield, Illinois.*

Lincoln's body was finally laid to rest at Oak Ridge Cemetery on the outskirts of Springfield, not downtown as the city's authorities had hoped. *Courtesy of Sangamon Valley Collection, Lincoln Library, Springfield, Illinois.*

predecessor, Richard Yates, to change her mind, Mary finally relented and chose Oak Ridge Cemetery on the north side of town for her husband's final resting place. It was a lovely, quiet place, filled with large oaks whose cool green leaves shaded rolling hills. It was also, the town elders decided, too far away from downtown. In life, Lincoln may have been their friend and colleague, but in death he was sure to be a tourist attraction, and the city authorities wanted to make sure that he was placed where visitors could see him. Near the Executive Mansion would be good; near the railroad tracks would be better.

Without consulting Mary or Robert Lincoln, the town's newly formed National Lincoln Monument Association (which included Lincoln's first law partner, John T. Stuart) set about constructing a marble vault on a tree-covered rise in the center of town in full view of the railroad station. When Mary got wind of their plans, she fired off an angry telegram from Washington, emphasizing her wish that Lincoln be buried at Oak Ridge. The National Lincoln Monument Association ignored her and went on with its work, carving "Abraham Lincoln" above the tomb and placing a matching pair of urns on each side as a finishing touch. But Mary Lincoln knew how to play hardball. Her next telegram flatly stated that "if her wishes and directions in regard to her husband's remains are not complied with she will move them to Chicago next June." Cowed, the association backed down, and the receiving vault at Oak Ridge was hastily fitted up in preparation for Lincoln's remains. It would take another telegram from Mary, this time threatening to take Lincoln's body to Washington to be buried under the dome of the Capitol Building, before the National Monument Association gave up its scheme for good.

The town that Lincoln returned to in death had changed dramatically since that April day nearly thirty years earlier when he first arrived to call Springfield his home. The cluster of dusty little wooden buildings housing fewer than 3,000 residents had blossomed into a sprawling grid of frame and brick houses and businesses, as well as a population that topped 12,000. One thing, however, had not changed: Springfield still had a penchant for wickedness that not even the somber occasion of Lincoln's funeral could stem. That day, as better than 150,000 people thronged the streets to pay their final respects to their friend and fallen leader, at least 19 pickpockets were working the crowds. Senator Henry Lane of Indiana was one of the victims.

BIBLIOGRAPHY

INTRODUCTION

Illinois Republican.

CHAPTER 1: POLITICAL BRAWLS

Fighting with Words

Miller, Richard Lawrence. *Lincoln and His World: The Early Years, Birth to the Illinois Legislature.* Mechanicsburg, PA: Stackpole Books, 2006.

Sangamo Journal.

Fighting with Fists

Basler, Roy P., et al. *Collected Works of Abraham Lincoln.* New Brunswick, NJ: Rutgers University Press, 1953.

Brown, Caroline Owsley. "Springfield Society before the Civil War." *Journal of the Illinois State Historical Society* 15 (1922–23): 477–500.

Brown, Christopher Columbus. "Major John T. Stuart." *Transactions of the Illinois State Historical Society.* Springfield, IL, 1902.

Davis, David. "Memorial Address: The Life and Services of John Todd Stuart." *Proceedings of the Illinois State Bar Association.* Springfield, IL, 1886.

History of Sangamon County. Chicago: Inter-State Publishing Company, 1881.
Sangamo Journal.

FIGHTING (FATALLY) WITH FIREARMS

Angle, Paul M. *Here I Have Lived: A History of Lincoln's Springfield, 1821–1865.* Chicago: Abraham Lincoln Book Shop, 1971.
Chicago Daily American.
Duff, John J. *A. Lincoln: Prairie Lawyer.* New York: Rinehart & Company, 1960.
Illinois State Journal.
Sangamo Journal.
Wilson, Douglas L., and Rodney O. Davis, eds. *Herndon's Informants: Letters, Interviews, and Statements about Abraham Lincoln.* Urbana: University of Illinois Press, 1998.

CHAPTER 2: GOVERNORS' (MIS)DEEDS

JOEL MATTESON AND THE GREAT CANAL SCRIP SCANDAL

Basler, Roy P., et al. *Collected Works of Abraham Lincoln.* New Brunswick, NJ: Rutgers University Press, 1953.
Hickey, James T. "An Illinois First Family: The Reminiscences of Clara Matteson Doolittle." *Journal of the Illinois State Historical Society* 69, no. 1 (1976): 2–16.
Howard, Robert P. *Mostly Good and Competent Men: Illinois Governors, 1818–1988.* Springfield: Illinois State Historical Society, 1988.
Illinois Reports, 1859.
Pease, Theodore, and James G. Randall, eds. *The Diary of Orville Hickman Browning.* Vol. 1, 1850–1864. Springfield: Illinois State Historical Library, 1925.
Pinsker, Matthew. "Senator Lincoln." *Journal of the Abraham Lincoln Association* 14, no. 2 (1993): 1–21.

WILLIAM H. BISSELL'S DUEL, DISINGENUOUSNESS AND DEBILITATING DISEASE

Bissell, William H. *The Slave Question: The Speech of Hon. Wm. H. Bissell, of Illinois, in the House of Representatives, Thursday, February 21, 1850.* Washington, D.C.: Buell & Blanchard, 1850.

Chamberlain, Samuel E. *My Confession.* New York: Harper & Brothers, 1956.

Gillespie Papers. Abraham Lincoln Presidential Library, Springfield, Illinois.

Snyder Papers. Abraham Lincoln Presidential Library, Springfield, Illinois.

Stowell, Daniel W., ed. *The Papers of Abraham Lincoln: Legal Documents and Cases.* 4 vols. Charlottesville: University of Virginia Press, 2008.

Trout, Jack R. "William H. Bissell: Anti-Nebraska Democrat and First Republican Governor of Illinois." Master's thesis, Illinois State University, 1862.

Winders, Richard Bruce. *Mr. Polk's Army: The American Military Experience in the Mexican War.* College Station: Texas A&M University Press, 1997. Reprint 2008.

CHAPTER 3: SEX, SLANDER AND FIGHTING

Etcheson, Nicole. "Manliness and the Political Culture of the Old Northwest." *Journal of the Early Republic* 15 (Spring 1995): 59–77.

Steiner, Mark E. *An Honest Calling: The Law Practice of Abraham Lincoln.* Dekalb: Northern Illinois University Press, 2006.

Stowell, Daniel W., ed. *In Tender Consideration: Women, Families, and the Law in Abraham Lincoln's Illinois.* Urbana: University of Illinois Press, 2002.

LOVERS, BROTHELS AND VENEREAL DISEASES

Benner, Martha, and Cullom Davis, eds. *The Law Practice of Abraham Lincoln: Complete Documentary Edition.* Urbana: University of Illinois, 2000.

SLANDEROUS STATEMENTS AND ATROCIOUS ACCUSATIONS

Benner, Martha, and Cullom Davis, eds. *The Law Practice of Abraham Lincoln: Complete Documentary Edition.* Urbana: University of Illinois, 2000.

FIGHTING DIRTY

Benner, Martha, and Cullom Davis, eds. *The Law Practice of Abraham Lincoln: Complete Documentary Edition.* Urbana: University of Illinois, 2000.

Gorn, Elliott J. "'Gouge and Bite, Pull Hair and Scratch': The Social Significance of Fighting in the Southern Backcountry." *American Historical Review* 90, no. 1 (February 1985): 18–43.

Nolte, Vincent. *Fifty Years in Both Hemispheres, or, Reminisces of the Life of a Former Merchant.* New York: Redfield, 1854.
Schob, David E. "Sodbusting on the Upper Midwest Frontier, 1820–1860." *Agricultural History* 47, no. 1 (January 1973): 47–56.

CHAPTER 4: SLAVERY IN THE EMANCIPATOR'S HOMETOWN

Hart, Richard E. *Lincoln's Springfield: The Early African American Population of Springfield, Illinois 1818–1861.* Spring Creek Series. Springfield, IL: self-published, 2008.

SPRINGFIELD'S SLAVES AND INDENTURED SERVANTS

Hart, Richard E. *Lincoln's Springfield: The Early African American Population of Springfield, Illinois 1818–1861.* Richard Hart: Spring Creek Series, 2008.
Herndon, William Henry. *Herndon's Life of Lincoln.* Edited by Paul M. Angle. Cleveland and New York: World Publishing Company, 1949.
Session minutes of the First Presbyterian Church of Springfield. Vol. 1, Abraham Lincoln Presidential Library.
Wilson, Douglas L., and Rodney O. Davis, eds. *Herndon's Informants: Letters, Interviews, and Statements about Abraham Lincoln.* Urbana: University of Illinois Press, 1998.

THE FUGITIVE SLAVE CASE

Benner, Martha, and Cullom Davis, eds. *The Law Practice of Abraham Lincoln: Complete Documentary Edition.* Urbana: University of Illinois, 2000.
Herndon-Parker Papers, University of Iowa.
Illinois State Journal.
Illinois State Register.

CHAPTER 5: ABRAHAM LINCOLN'S SCANDAL

THE POISON PEN

Donald, David Herbert. *Lincoln.* New York: Simon & Schuster, 1995.
Sangamo Journal.

Wilson, Douglas L., and Rodney O. Davis, eds. *Herndon's Informants: Letters, Interviews, and Statements about Abraham Lincoln*. Urbana: University of Illinois Press, 1998.

THE DUEL

Basler, Roy P., et al. *Collected Works of Abraham Lincoln*. New Brunswick, NJ: Rutgers University Press, 1953.

Burlingame, Michael, ed. *Oral History of Abraham Lincoln: John G. Nicolay's Interviews and Essays*. Carbondale: Southern Illinois University Press, 1996.

Carpenter, Francis. *Six Months in the White House with Abraham Lincoln: The Story of a Picture.* New York: Hurd and Houghton, 1867.

Linder, Usher F. *Reminiscences of the Early Bench and Bar of Illinois*. Chicago: Chicago Legal News Company, 1879.

Rothschild, Alonzo. *Lincoln: Master of Men*. Boston: Houghton Mifflin & Co., 1906.

Sangamo Journal.

CHAPTER 6: MURDER MOST FOUL

THE TRAILOR MYSTERY: THE MURDER THAT WASN'T

Basler, Roy P., et al. *Collected Works of Abraham Lincoln*. New Brunswick, NJ: Rutgers University Press, 1953.

Benner, Martha, and Cullom Davis, eds. *The Law Practice of Abraham Lincoln: Complete Documentary Edition*. Urbana: University of Illinois, 2000.

Quincy Whig.

Sangamo Journal.

BUMPED OFF IN THE BACKYARD

Benner, Martha, and Cullom Davis, eds. *The Law Practice of Abraham Lincoln: Complete Documentary Edition*. Urbana: University of Illinois, 2000.

Fenster, Julie. *The Case of Abraham Lincoln: A Story of Adultery, Murder, and the Making of a Great President*. New York: Palgrave Macmillan, 2007.

Illinois State Journal.

Illinois State Register.

Linder, Usher F. *Reminiscences of the Early Bench and Bar of Illinois*. Chicago: Chicago Legal News Company, 1879.
Missouri Republican.

A Shot in the Dark

Benner, Martha, and Cullom Davis, eds. *The Law Practice of Abraham Lincoln: Complete Documentary Edition*. Urbana: University of Illinois, 2000.
Illinois State Journal.
Unpublished manuscript, Lincoln Collection, Photostat collection, Abraham Lincoln Presidential Library.

Infanticide of an Illegitimate Child

Benner, Martha, and Cullom Davis, eds. *The Law Practice of Abraham Lincoln: Complete Documentary Edition*, Urbana: University of Illinois, 2000.
Illinois State Journal.
Illinois State Register.

A Dance Turns Deadly

Benner, Martha, and Cullom Davis, eds. *The Law Practice of Abraham Lincoln: Complete Documentary Edition*. Urbana: University of Illinois, 2000.
Illinois State Journal.
Illinois State Register.

CHAPTER 7: CIVIL WAR SHENANIGANS

"History: Camp Butler National Cemetery," Unpublished manuscript, Sangamon Valley Collection, Lincoln Library, Springfield, Illinois.
McAndrew, Tara McClellan. "Camp Misery: Medicine was Sparse at Badly Overcrowded Camp Butler." *Illinois Times*, May 15, 2008.

Revelry and Riots

History of Sangamon County. Chicago: Inter-State Publishing Company, 1881.
Illinois State Journal.

AN OFFICER WITH A HAIR-TRIGGER TEMPER

History of Sangamon County. Chicago: Inter-State Publishing Company, 1881.

Illinois State Journal.

SHOT BY A SOLDIER IN THE STREET

Benner, Martha, and Cullom Davis, eds. *The Law Practice of Abraham Lincoln: Complete Documentary Edition*. Urbana: University of Illinois, 2000.

History of Sangamon County, 1881. Chicago: Inter-State Publishing Company.

Illinois State Journal.

LINCOLN'S WARTIME NEPOTISM GONE BAD

Basler, Roy P., et al. *Collected Works of Abraham Lincoln*. New Brunswick, NJ: Rutgers University Press, 1953.

Lincoln Papers, Library of Congress.

Wilson, Douglas L., and Rodney O. Davis, eds. *Herndon's Informants: Letters, Interviews, and Statements about Abraham Lincoln*. Urbana: University of Illinois Press, 1998.

EPILOGUE

Craughwell, Thomas J. *Stealing Lincoln's Body*. Cambridge, MA: Harvard University Press, 2007.

Illinois State Journal.

Kunhardt, Dorothy Meserve, and Philip B. Kunhardt Jr. *Twenty Days: A Narrative in Text and Pictures of the Assassination of Abraham Lincoln and the Twenty Days and Nights that followed—The Nation in Mourning, the Long Trip Home to Springfield*. North Hollywood, CA: Newcastle Publishing Co., 1985.

ABOUT THE AUTHOR

Courtesy of Michael Gowin Photography.

Erika Holst holds a master's degree from the Winterthur Program in Early American Culture. She has volunteered, interned and worked at museums and history projects throughout Illinois, including the David Davis Mansion State Historic Site in Bloomington, the McLean County Museum of History in Bloomington, the Cuneo Museum in Vernon Hills, Dickson Mounds Museum in Lewistown, the Papers of Abraham Lincoln, the Illinois State Museum and the Abraham Lincoln Presidential Library in Springfield.